THE

REVELATION OF THE FATHER.

THE

REVELATION OF THE FATHER:

SHORT LECTURES

ON

THE TITLES OF THE LORD

IN THE

GOSPEL OF ST JOHN.

BROOKE FOSS WESTCOTT, D.D. D.C.L.

REGIUS PROFESSOR OF DIVINITY, AND FELLOW OF
KING'S COLLEGE, CAMBRIDGE.

Eugene, Oregon

Wipf and Stock Publishers
199 W 8th Ave, Suite 3
Eugene, OR 97401

The Revelation of the Father
Short Lectures on the Titles of the Lord in the Gospel of St. John
By Westcott, B.F.
ISBN: 1-59244-863-1
Publication date 9/14/2004
Previously published by Macmillan, 1884

PREFACE.

IT was my intention to deliver the substance of these lectures during my Summer residence at Peterborough in the present year. Very shortly before the time of residence came my connexion with the Cathedral was most unexpectedly broken and my purpose was consequently unfulfilled. I have reason however to think that some to whom I had been allowed to minister for fourteen Summers, would have followed with interest the examination of a subject which we had already approached eleven years ago, and it has been a pleasure to me to continue so far as I could the old relation by revising week after week what I had hoped to address to them. Such friends will, I trust, receive the result as a memorial of a connexion on which I shall always look back with affectionate gratitude.

W.

The subject itself is one to which I was anxious to direct attention. A complete series of related passages of Holy Scripture taken just as they stand without the exercise of any choice presents, as I believe, with incomparable clearness that harmonious progress of thought in the record of divine revelation which makes the idea of inspiration a living reality.

This is true especially of the narratives of the Gospels. And no one, unless I am mistaken, can consider the titles by which the Lord successively reveals Himself in the Gospel of St John without acknowledging the naturalness of each revelation, and the growing light which they throw one after the other in due order upon His work and upon His Person. Each title as it was used was intelligible. Each title when studied afterwards disclosed (and still discloses) fuller depths of meaning. On the other hand there is not the least indication that this vital unfolding of the truth little by little, these underlying correspondences, were directly present to the mind of the Evangelist as he wrote, still less that they were due to a conscious design. We observe them only when we allow every detail of time and place and circumstance to produce its full effect through patient medita-

Preface.

tion. In this respect what I have said can only suggest topics for meditation and not supersede the exercise itself.

Such meditation will bring back with a multiplied blessing that complete trust in the Written Word, quickened by the Living Word, which many seem to mourn over as irreparably lost. No doubt we have used the Scriptures for purposes for which they were not designed. We have treated them too often as the one mechanical utterance of the Spirit and not as writings through which the Spirit Himself still speaks. We have isolated them from the life of the Christian society, and that still larger life which is, in its measure, a manifestation of God. There is an immeasurable difference between making the Bible a storehouse of formal premisses from which doctrinal systems can be infallibly constructed and making it in its whole fulness the final test of necessary Truth. The Bible itself teaches us by its antithetic utterances that no single expression of the Truth is coextensive with the Truth itself. And life proves beyond question that words gather wealth in the course of the ages. It is not too much to say that no formula which expresses clearly the thought of one generation can convey the same meaning to the generation which follows. It may happily express a commensurate meaning, but every term in which the meaning is conveyed will have gained new associations.

And it is in this that the divine power of Holy Scripture makes itself most powerfully felt by the student. The language of the Bible grows more harmoniously luminous with the growing light. When its words are read and interpreted simply, as words still living, they are found to give the spiritual message which each age requires, the one message made audible to each hearer in the language wherein he was born.

The series of self-revelations of the Lord which are examined in the following lectures serve in this sense to illustrate the Inspiration of the Bible. They serve also to illustrate another momentous problem which occupies the minds of many. Few who strive to realise the events of the Gospel as an actual history can fail to have asked themselves, with something of trembling fear, how we can conceive that the disciples who had followed the Lord during His ministry, as men following One who was true Man, came to realise His Divine Nature. The first nine chapters of the Acts of the Apostles, with their marvellous picture of growing perception called out by the Spirit though simple events, when studied in the light of these revelations go far to make the result intelligible from the human side. One fact, one truth after another is welcomed and appropriated. All alike point in the same direction: all finally converge in a central supreme fact, a central supreme truth, by which they are harmonized. There is no abrupt transition, no violent passage from one mode of thought to another. Elements of infinity gather round the Lord, and He is seen at last to stand before the soul in His full glory.

I have added as an Appendix to the lectures three Sermons preached at Cambridge, in which I have endeavoured to state in greater detail and in a somewhat different form one or two main conclusions to which the line of thought followed in the lectures seems to point. These conclusions are to me full of encouragement even if they call for great exertion *lest haply we drift away from them*. If we can come to live as knowing that divine voices are addressed to us, that divine truth is being shaped through us, that we have entrusted to our keeping that which grows with the accumulated growth of every human faculty and all human progress, we shall rate our trials at their due value.

The words with which St Paul prefaced a view of nature and history which we are just beginning to understand come back to us with overmastering force: *I reckon that the sufferings of this present time are not worthy to be compared with the glory which shall be revealed to us-ward.*

B. F. W.

Thun,
September 12, 1883.

CONTENTS.

I.

THE COMING IN THE FATHER'S NAME.

	PAGE
The revelation through Christ's titles a clue to the apprehension of the Incarnation	3
offered for our guidance	4
Christ comes in the Father's Name.	
1. The Name	5
in connexion with divine revelation El-Shaddai; Jehovah; Jehovah-Sabáoth: silence	6
How significant permanently	7
Illustration from Ps. xix.	8
2. The Father's Name.	
A gift of the Gospel	9
Earlier strivings after fellowship with God	id.
end in an insoluble antithesis	10
Christ harmonises the two antithetic truths	id.
He revealed the Father	11
3. Coming in the Father's Name	
A declaration of Sonship	id.
self-surrender	12
love	id.
These revelations for common use	13

II.

THE CHRIST.

	PAGE
The technical sense of the title 'Messiah' 'Christ' post-Biblical .	17
Compared with the 'Word'	18
The title Christ the revelation of the Divine patience	19
The purpose of God slowly and partially made known	20
Through the patriarchs; the family .	21
theocracy : the nation .	22
kingdom : the king	23
captivity : the servant .	id.
return .	24
The issue at the Coming of the Son of Man in partial knowledge .	id.
The teaching of the title now	
waiting	26
watching .	id.
hoping	27
The peculiarity of the revelation to a Samaritan woman .	28

III.

THE BREAD OF LIFE.

The revelation at Capernaum a test of faith .	31
The fundamental revelation of life .	32
1. The fact of life	
The occasion of the revelation .	33
The revelation corrects and transfigures the imperfect conception of the Jews	34
It answers to a human need	35
2. The support of life	
Prepared by a vital energy	36
for action and for rest .	37
'The bread of life' is also 'living bread;' and .	38

	PAGE
'the flesh' of Christ	39
by which we are united with Him	id.
3. The appropriation of spiritual food.	
'Eating the flesh' of Christ the highest energy of faith	40
A vital incorporation	id.
Relation to the Holy Eucharist and to life	41
The present power of the revelation	42

IV.

THE LIGHT OF THE WORLD.

The lessons of the Feast of Tabernacles	47
The water and the light	48
The connexion of the revelation	49
The general idea of light	50
Light a revelation of hidden beauty	51
So Christ the Interpreter of Creation	id.
Light reveals and does not make darkness	52
So Christ has made evil felt by a Presence of perfect light	id.
The unity and purity of light presented in Christ	53
reflected in the unity of the Church	id.
Light self-attested	54
Even so Christ	id.
The light given for use	55
The Disciples of Christ are also 'the light of the world'	57

V.

THE DOOR OF THE SHEEP.

The titles 'the Door' and 'the Good Shepherd' mark a special relation	63
The circumstances under which they were announced	65
The allegory of the sheepfold	66
Two thoughts: the fold and the flock	id.

Contents.

	PAGE
Christ the Door of the sheep	67
The general idea of a fold	68
foreign to modern thought	id.
but essentially Christian	id.
The blessing of outward fellowship	69
The position of a Christian one of security	id.
through Christ he enters on new relations to man and God	70
From this position he 'goes out' to win the world, and	71
'finds pasture' there, and returns when work is over	72
The lesson for us	73

VI.

THE GOOD SHEPHERD.

A summary view of Christ's work as the Door of the sheep	77
Christ as the Good Shepherd, the earliest and most universal image	78
The image in the Old Testament	79
The prayer of Moses fulfilled in Christ	id.
The aspects of the Shepherd's office.	
Absolute Devotion	80
Perfect Sympathy	id.
Christ gave a new ideal of leadership and of discipleship	81
He claimed the strayed sheep as still His own, and	82
in this He differed from 'the hireling'.	83
He gave His life for those entrusted to Him	id.
This devotion rests on knowledge	84
which is the foundation of sympathy and coexists with love	id.
Knowledge answers to knowledge	85
The relation rests on a divine relation	id.
True government shewn in the work of the Good Shepherd	86
Our work	87

VII.

THE RESURRECTION AND THE LIFE.

	PAGE
The first and last signs test and quicken faith	91
The raising of Lazarus shews Christ as the Resurrection and the Life	92
Christ turns all thought upon Himself	id.
In the presence of death He makes known His power	93
The Resurrection and the Life present blessings	94
The history of the raising a revelation of death and life	95
The Resurrection and the Life not only through Christ but in Christ	96
This revelation a mystery which we can see only dimly	97
All that is is life in Christ	id.
Man cannot separate himself from the universe	98
nor from his fellow men	id.
The life of all is Christ	99
Hence St Paul's phrase 'in Christ'	id.
The fulness of personal life preserved in this universal life	id.
'Believest thou this?'	100
The beginning and growth of faith	101

VIII.

THE WAY, THE TRUTH, AND THE LIFE.

The two last revelations of the Lord given to the Eleven only	105
'Arise, let us go hence'	106
The question of St Thomas	108
The Lord's answer meets all the fears of His disciples.	
He is the Way through the world in which they are to be left	id.

Contents.

	PAGE
He is the Truth which survives all change	109
He is the Life even on the Cross	id.
This answer is for us also	110
In our hurried and restless perplexity Christ reveals Himself as the Way	111
In the shaking of traditional beliefs He reveals Himself as the Truth	112
In the overpowering pressure of outward things He reveals Himself as the Life	113
Christ's power active even when not recognised	114
To us all it is shewn plainly	115

IX.

THE TRUE VINE.

The revelation of Christ through the image of the Vine combines former revelations and fulfils teaching of the Old Testament	119
The life in Christ is manifold	120
The parts of the Vine individually different though in origin ideally the same	122
All required for its fruitful life	id.
No rivalry, no comparison between their diversities	123
The life in Christ is one	124
The Vine includes all the present parts and all the past in one life	id.
The past lives in the present	125
The life in Christ is fruitful	126
The Vine is not a wild tree	id.
Its fruitfulness is the necessary result of its training	id.
The life thus manifested is the life of Christ	127
Hence come confidence, strength, hope	128
Perfected through discipline	id.

X.

THE VISION OF CHRIST, THE VISION OF THE FATHER.

	PAGE
The manifold revelations of Christ form a revelation of the Father	133
The history of man and men is naturally a history of the withdrawal of God from the world	134
The history of Israel a parable of individual religious growth, Covenant: Law: Prophecy: Silence: the Revelation of the Father	id.
The Father's patience.	
The Christ: the Word	137
The Father's love	138
Gives life	139
light	id.
shelter (the Door)	id.
confidence (the Good Shepherd)	140
resurrection	id.
The Father's discipline.	
We come to Him only through Christ	id.
He is the Husbandman	141
In Christ God is given back to us as the object of human affections and faith	142

APPENDIX I.

THE TESTIMONY OF JESUS THE SPIRIT OF PROPHECY.

The testimony of Jesus the spirit of prophecy	148
The spirit of prophecy the testimony of Jesus	149
The history and the record of the history of the Jews unique	150

xviii *Contents.*

	PAGE
The spirit of the Old Testament	151
The idea expressed in the record of Creation, and	152
the Call of Abraham	153
This was set out in the life of the nation.	154
The whole life of Israel preparatory for the Gospel.	156
which alone completes it.	157
The importance of regarding the Old Testament in this light	158

APPENDIX II.

The Revelation of the Glory of God: the Annunciation and the Resurrection.

The idea of the Glory of God in the Bible	164
The Glory of God revealed through Israel, and	166
through 'the Servant of the Lord'.	167
This Glory shewn in the human Life of Christ	168
The Life of Christ continued in the life of the Church and of believers	170
The combination of the Festivals of the Annunciation and Easter offers the fulness of hope	172

APPENDIX III.

The Revelation of the Triune God an Implicit Gospel.

Trinity Sunday the Festival of Revelation	177
The Revelation of God offered to us	179
to be apprehended gradually	180
We pass from the action of God to the being of God	181

	PAGE
The conception of the Triune God illuminates the fact of the Creation, and	182
of the Incarnation	183
It gives a stable unity to life	id.
The conception practical	184
a true Gospel	186
verified in its effects	id.

I.

THE COMING IN THE FATHER'S NAME.

I am come in my Father's name.

St John v. 43.

IN the course of these lectures I propose to consider some of the great lessons which are revealed to us in the Titles of the Lord contained in the Gospel of St John. It may be that if we take them one by one, just as they are presented to us in the divine narrative; if we strive to enter a little more fully into their meaning than we commonly do; if we regard them in their connexion with one another and with the lines of thought and history to which they correspond, we shall learn something more of those open secrets which are scattered throughout the Bible, and so gain fresh strength to do our appointed work. It may be that we shall be enabled to perceive with a more vital intelligence how in the progress of natural intercourse the disciples received those lessons through which they afterwards apprehended the Divine Majesty of their Master, and so gain for ourselves a more present sense of the Incarnation. In this direction, as it appears to me, we have a work to do. For again and again I would remind all who may hear me, as I wish to be reminded myself, that Holy Scripture is unexhausted and inexhaustible: that all later knowledge is as a commentary which guides us further into the true understanding of prophets, apostles and evangelists: that through old forms, old words, old thoughts—old and yet new—the Spirit of God speaks to us with a voice never before clearly intelligible as *we* can hear it: that it is our duty and our joy to ponder all that has been written for our learning, knowing that each mysterious character will grow luminous to the eye of faith. In these times more than ever before we need patience at every turn and we need wisdom: the patience which is content to wait for truth, and the wisdom which welcomes truths half-reconciled. So may God in His great love grant to us an access of these blessings—wiser patience, more patient wisdom—through the inquiry on which we are entering. And let us not doubt: as we ask, He will give, and give more than we ask.

But before we begin to examine the titles of the Lord I wish to call attention to the words in which the Lord Himself describes the general character of His manifestation: *I am come in my Father's name.* For it will be in the light of this central revelation that all partial revelations must be viewed. Each separate title will thus help us in due proportion to apprehend the great sum of all, and prepare us to grasp as a fact, deep and broad as life, the declaration with which Christ crowned His work: *He that hath seen me hath seen the Father.*

I am come in my Father's name. The sense which common usage attaches to the words, as if Christ said only 'I am come as my Father's representative, speaking with His authority, charged with His Message,' falls far short of their true significance. They imply yet further that Christ claims to act, speak, live in God made known as the Father: that His works are wrought in the Father: that He is not separate from the Father but One with Him. The exact opposite of the phrase is that which is immediately contrasted with it here, 'the coming in one's own name,' standing, that is, alone, self-sustained, self-reliant, isolated in a human personality, moved by individual wishes and motives.

This fuller meaning of the words will be seen more clearly if we consider them in detail, step by step, (1) the name, (2) the Father's name, (3) the coming in the Father's name.

1. Every thoughtful reader of the Bible must have been often struck by the importance which is attached to the Divine Names in the different Books. When Jacob wrestled with the Angel till the break of day and prevailed, his last prayer to his heavenly antagonist was *Tell me, I*

pray Thee, Thy name. When Moses received the commission to deliver Israel from Egypt, he found his credentials in the new name of God: *God spake unto Moses and said unto him: I am the* LORD *(Jehovah); and I appeared unto Abraham, unto Isaac, and unto Jacob, by the name of God Almighty, but by my name Jehovah was I not known to them.* When Zechariah looked out beyond the darkness of the exile and saw the dawning glory of the day of the Lord, he gathered up in one sentence the consummation of all hope: *In that day shall there be one Lord, and His name one.*

Gen. xxxii. 29.

Ex. vi. 2 ff.

Zech. xiv. 9.

It is indeed not too much to say that the three chief stages in the History of the Old Testament are characterised in broad outline by the names under which God was pleased to make Himself known in each. First He was known as *El-Shaddai*, the God of might, rich in blessing and powerful in judgment, when He sought to create and cherish in the patriarchs the sense of personal dependence upon a strong helper. Then He was known as *Jehovah*, the Eternal who makes Himself known in time, One and unchangeable, when a sacred people had to be fashioned out of a host of fugitive slaves by ennobling relationship with an infinite spiritual power. Then at last He was known as the Lord of Hosts, *Jehovah Sabáoth*, when the vicissitudes of national life had given to the people *in the Old Testament.* 7

some experience of the wider providential government of the world[1].

We may go yet one step further. When the teaching of the prophets was ended, and men were left for a time, as it seemed, to themselves, the divine name of revelation was unspoken and unread. A blank took the place of what was the pledge of God's love; and superstitious fear was substituted for loyal reverence. At first sight this singular significance, this mysterious virtue attached to the divine name may appear strange, but if we pause for a moment we shall see whence it comes. Of God as He is in Himself, in His absolute and unapproachable Majesty, we can as yet know nothing. But the names by which we are allowed to address Him gather up what is shewn to us, relatively to our powers, of His working and of His will. The divine names receive and reflect scattered rays of heavenly truth as men can bear their effulgence; and when they have been set in our spiritual firmament they burn for ever. Thus each name authoritatively given to God is, so to speak, a fresh and lasting revelation of His nature. Now

[1] The general sense in which the Sacred Names are used is given truly, I believe, in these sentences; but I do not offer any opinion on the actual derivation of the Names themselves. It happens constantly, I believe, that names borrowed from a foreign source are interpreted and used according to likenesses in sound to words familiar to the people who have borrowed them.

1. in one title and now in another we catch glimpses of His ineffable glory. Each one in turn becomes a beacon to guide us, a pathway of light traversing the world of thought. And if we would penetrate at all to the deeper meanings of Scripture we must watch heedfully for the interchange of the divine names in which long trains of argument or reflection are contained.   To take one example only. Throughout the book of the Psalms there is a marked contrast between two names, God, *Elohim*, the God of Nature, and the LORD, *Jehovah*, the God of the Covenant. When we bear this in mind familiar words gain a new force. We then know, and not till then, how it is that David can begin a Psalm with the stirring words *The heavens declare the glory of God*, while his eyes are still fixed upon the magnificence of creation: and how it is that at the last, conscious of weakness and sin, he closes it with a trustful prayer *to the LORD his strength and his Redeemer*.

Ps. xix. 1.

Ps. xix. 14.

2. The particular name of God then which is used in any case suggests as an element of thought that special aspect of the Divine nature which the name itself symbolises or expresses. With this truth present to us, we can now go on to consider what is involved in 'the Father's name.'   The ideas of power, of majesty, of leadership, of unutterable awe, which had been before connected with Deity, are in that merged in the idea of tender personal relationship. So

the Father.

at last in the fulness of time the connexion which had been established with a patriarch, with a family, with a nation, on the basis of absolute authority, was revealed to exist, at once more widely and more individually, in the essential bond by which mankind was united to Him who had created and redeemed them.

The name of the Father. That new name is characteristic of the Gospel. *The hour cometh and now is, when the true worshippers shall worship the Father....*So Christ spoke for the first time. The name of Father is indeed the sum of the Christian revelation: into that name we are all baptized: the hallowing of that name is the subject of our first prayer. For ages men had longed to call God 'Father', but the aspiration appeared to be a vague and visionary hope. They strove to divest themselves in imagination of all that is material and mortal, if so be that some unsubstantial spirit might be left not wholly alien from a divine kindred. They unclothed themselves, to use St Paul's expressive image, of all that belongs to the fulness of personal life, that even so, shadowy and phantomlike, they might be admitted to a heavenly fellowship. The passionate craving remained when every attempt to satisfy it failed. It seemed as if God were withdrawn more and more from the world as experience gave precision to thought, and yet men

John iv.23.

2 Cor. v. 4.

clung to the belief that they were indeed His offspring. They knew that God only could know God. They knew that man only could be touched with the feeling for man's infirmities. In the face of this final contradiction they hoped still; and the hope was not vain.

Christ, the Son of God, the Son of Man, reconciled what had been held to be irreconcileable. As Son of God, He knew the Father perfectly. As Son of man He revealed the Father perfectly. In His own Person He offered the supreme proof of the Father's love by taking man's nature upon earth. In His own Person He offered the supreme pledge of man's divine sonship by raising his nature to heaven. In a word he declared the Father's name: He declared that we are not simply poor, frail creatures of a day, but heirs of an eternal inheritance. He declared that helpless, erring, sinstained as we are, we can yet be brought back, cleansed through His blood, to our true home: He declared that in Him we too even now may see the Father.

The name of the Father—the knowledge of God that is, as watching over, drawing to Himself, guiding, loving all men and each man particularly, as binding the whole family of the human race to one another by natural ties of ineffaceable kinsmanship, as calling them to the full enjoyment of their spiritual birthright as His sons—this

Christ has brought to us. At the close of His open ministry, His petition was *Father glorify Thy name*. When He reviewed His work in His last high-priestly prayer He said: *Father I manifested...I made known Thy name [to them whom Thou hast given me] and I will make it known, that the love wherewith thou lovedst me may be in them and I in them*. Upon the cross He added to the cry of David the title which spoke of trust in supreme agony *Father into Thy hands I commend my spirit*. And when the victory was won, He raised human affection to a loftier aim by the words: *Cling not to me for I am not yet ascended to my Father...I ascend unto my Father and your Father, and my God and your God*.

_{1.}
John xii. 28.
John xvii. 6, 26.
Ps. xxii. 1; Matt. xxvii. 46.
Luke xxiii. 46.
John xx. 17.

3. Thus at length we are brought to a fuller understanding of the whole phrase *I am come in my Father's name*. The advent of Christ was fulfilled that in Him men might learn to know His Father and their Father: that in Him they might learn to know the sovereignty of sacrifice: that in Him they might learn to know the infinity of love.

I am come in my Father's name. The words are a lesson of divine Sonship. If Christ be Son, then we who are in Christ are sons also. That relationship does not depend upon any precarious exercise of our own choice. We do not determine our parentage. We are children of a

12   *The revelation*

I.   heavenly Father by His will; and in that fact lies
confidence which no failure can annul.

I am come in my Father's name. The words
are a lesson of self-surrender. Christ
wrought and spoke only that men might know
John v. 19. His Father better. *The Son* He said *can do
nothing of himself but what He seeth the Father do.*
John xii. *Whatsoever I speak even as the Father hath said*
50.
John x. 30. *unto me so I speak. I and the Father are one.*
He veiled His own glory if it turned the eyes of
men from the glory of the Father. He refused
the homage which misinterpreted His mission.
As He gave us the assurance of Sonship, He
gave us also the example of Sonship.

I am come in my Father's name. The words
are a lesson of boundless love. Christ crowned
His life of sacrifice upon the Cross. Even from
this He revealed the Father when it seemed that
He was alone. In His desolation He shewed
as men could not otherwise have seen how *the
John iii. Father gave His only Son* for us: how *with Him
16.
Rom. viii. He will freely give us all things.* Thus the
32.   Incarnation of Christ sets forth the reality of our
sonship: the life of Christ sets forth the duties of
our sonship: the Passion of Christ sets forth,
so that we tremble when we regard them, the
privileges of our Sonship.

I am come in my Father's name. As the
weeks go on we may be allowed to see some frag-

ments of this revelation in greater detail. Meanwhile it may be well if we can carry with us to our daily work thoughts from this wider view. If we are depressed by continual failure, if we seem to stand idle as the hours go by, if our efforts seem to bring no fruit, let us forget ourselves: let us go back to the beginning of our Christian life: let us plead the promise of our Covenant, sure that God is waiting to accomplish what He has already begun: 'Father into Thy name we were baptized: give us the tenderness, the devotion, the trust of sons.'

If we are perplexed by the results and claims of physical or historical investigations, if opinions which have been handed down to us from early times appear to be no longer tenable, if we have to readjust our interpretation of the facts of Faith: let us welcome the truths which are established as revelations offered to meet the requirements of a later age, untroubled by the hasty deductions which are made from them: let us welcome them with the earliest petition which we learnt to make: *Our Father, hallowed be Thy Name;* may every fresh discovery in the order of nature and in the life of men be so accepted as to shew more of Thy Glory *of Whom every fatherhood in heaven and on earth is named.* [Eph. iii. 15.]

If we are distressed by strife and self-seeking, if jealousies and divisions hinder the progress and mar the glory of the Church, if rivalry and ambition disturb the great family of nations, let us hold fast the truth which outlives the storms of earth: let us concentrate in one energy of supplication all the thoughts of our common brotherhood: let us offer up unweariedly the prayer which Christ hath taught us in His fellowship and by His strength—Father, *our Father*,—that last best name, which gives to the ear of faith a promise of union underlying all differences and reaching beyond all time, of union which is established and not broken by death, of union which is consummated in the open vision of God.

II.

THE CHRIST.

The woman saith unto him, I know that Messiah cometh (which is called Christ); when he is come, he will declare unto us all things. Jesus saith unto her, I that speak unto thee am he.

St JOHN iv. 25, 26.

IT is remarkable that the title 'Messiah' ('Christ') which the Lord first definitely accepted as describing His office belonged in this sense specially to the post-Biblical age. In the Scriptures of the Old Testament the title of 'the Messiah,' 'the Christ,' 'the Anointed' had a wide application but it was not the special title of the promised Deliverer. It marked generally one who had been endowed with a divine gift for the fulfilment of a divine office. The High Priest and the King were thus characteristically spoken of as 'the Anointed.' This wider application of the word Messiah witnesses to a manifold action of God, fitting men for the accomplishment of His purpose in regard to humanity. All limited offices, all partial endowments of earlier 'Christs' were so presented as to become preparatory foreshadowings of 'the Christ,' in whom every work of prophet, priest and king found complete and harmonious consummation.

II.   The force of the title is seen most clearly when it is contrasted with that of the 'Word' which St John himself chooses to express his own thought. By speaking of the Lord as 'the Word,' the 'Logos,' he opens to us such a view as we are able to bear of the diversity of Persons in the timeless, absolute existence of the Godhead: he teaches us to regard all creation as springing directly from the divine will and all life as centreing in the divine presence: he encourages us to embrace the great truth that in all ages and in all lands God holds converse with His children, and that through all darkness and

John i. 9. all desolation a light shineth which lighteth every man.

This title the *Word* presents the Person of the Lord to us, if I may so express it, spiritually, as corresponding to the highest thoughts of man, from its divine side. The title, the *Messiah*, the *Christ*, gives the converse picture; and presents the Person of the Lord to us historically, as corresponding to the outward life of man, from its human side.

The Word describes One who is coeternal and coessential with God: the Christ describes One who has been invested by God with a special character.

The conception of the Word rises beyond time: the conception of the Christ is definitely realised in time.

The doctrine of the Word answers in a certain sense to the very constitution of man and belongs

to all humanity: the doctrine of the Christ is II.
slowly shaped by revelation and belongs to the
chosen people.

But while we recognise, and dwell upon, and
strive to give a practical reality to these differences,
we must remember that the two natures, the two
conceptions, the two doctrines are reconciled and
fulfilled in one Person. They stand side by side in
the first confession of personal faith which St John
has recorded—when Nathanael said to Him who
had read his inmost thoughts: *Rabbi, thou art the* John i. 49.
Son of God, thou art king of Israel: and they are
united for ever in the one phrase in which the
Evangelist sums up our Creed: *The Word became* John i. 14.
flesh.

Bearing this in mind we can now turn our
thoughts to the familiar title 'Christ.' The doctrine of the Messiah, the Christ, the Anointed One
was, as I have said, wrought out little by little in
many parts and in many fashions under the Old
Covenant. And it is in this fact that we find the
most precious lesson which the doctrine still
contains for us. If the thought of Christ as the
Word fills us with courage, the thought of the
Word as Christ fills us with patience.   It
cannot have been for nothing that God was pleased
to disclose His counsels, fragment by fragment, Hebr. i. 1.
through long intervals of silence and disappointment and disaster. In that slow preparation for
the perfect revelation of Himself to men which

The revelation of

II. was most inadequately apprehended till it was finally given, we discern the pattern of His ways. As it was in the case of the first Advent, even so now He is guiding the course of the world to the second Advent. We can see enough in the past, to find a vantage ground for faith; and, when the night is deepest and all sight fails, shall we not still *endure,* like the men of old time, *as seeing the invisible?*

Hebr. xi. 27.

This priceless lesson of divine patience which flows from the scriptural revelation of the Christ cannot, I think, be missed if we bear in mind the epochs and the general character of the rare and dark Messianic prophecies. By combining isolated passages of the Old Testament we commonly get a very false impression of the extent to which the hope of a personal Messiah is spread through them. By throwing back the light of the Truth which we know upon dark riddles, we dissipate the mystery in which they were at first shrouded. For indeed the teaching of the Law, the Psalms, and the Prophets in this respect is strangely different from what we should have expected. A few scattered hints here and there sufficient to witness to the continuity of the Divine purpose but not to display it: promises suited to support faith but not to satisfy it: types intelligible only as they answered to real cravings of the soul: such were the means by which God disciplined His ancient people for the coming

the Divine patience.

Saviour; such are the means by which He disciplines us. _{II.}

This will be clear if we recal in briefest outline the history of the Old Testament. The first distinct intimation of future blessing for mankind is found in the call of Abraham, for the dim, general prospect of victory, opened after the record of the Fall, cannot come into account here. That call is the starting-point of the history of the Church, through which, as time flows on, God is pleased to make Himself known. In Abraham a people was marked out to stand among the nations of the world as representatives of faith in a present accessible God. The sign by which it was sealed was self-sacrifice.   This primal revelation made to Abraham was solemnly repeated to Isaac and to Jacob. And these patriarchs, contented to remain strangers and pilgrims in a land which they knew to be their own by a heavenly title, looked for *the city which hath the foundations*, and so fulfilled their work.

Gen. xii. 2, 3.

Gen. xxvi. 4; xxviii. 14.

Hebr. xi. 9, 10, 13, ff.

The age of the patriarchs was followed by the age of the Law.

A bondage of two hundred years uncheered, as far as we know, and unenlightened by any fresh promise could not destroy altogether what had been taught to Israel by God's covenant with their fathers. A nation had grown up, to whom the name of the God of Abraham and Isaac and Jacob was still a spell of sacred power. But when they received the Law, they received as yet no clear revelation of a personal Saviour. They were indeed to look for a prophet, some greater Moses, who should teach what Moses had left unsaid, but they were themselves to be the messengers of God, and God Himself was to be their king. In them all the nations of the earth were to find blessing, that is in the obedience, the purity, the faith, which were the springs of their common life.

<small>Deut. xviii. 18.</small>

We all know the sad story of the Jewish Theocracy. The Law made clear the weakness and the sinfulness of man. The people refused to rest under the protection of an unseen Ruler. In terrible reverses, in signal victories, they realised the anger and the mercy of Jehovah; but as they did so, they came to feel the need of some one who should stand between them and that supreme Majesty. They asked for an earthly king. The function of the Messianic nation, so to speak, was devolved upon a personal Messiah. The age of the Law was followed by the age of the Kingdom.

At this point then the divine promises take a new form. The blessing which had before been connected with a people was now connected with a Prince. The reign of David created new hopes which it could not fulfil. The service of the fixed Temple, which naturally followed, brought the offices and the thoughts of religion into nearer connexion with civil life. Men felt, by the help of these earthly images, as they had not II. done before, the power of a divine government and a divine presence. And the Holy Spirit speaking through the prophets used these symbols to give distinctness to their pictures of the future triumph of Jehovah. The very name Messiah— Ps. ii. 2. the Lord's Anointed—which was now used in this sense for the first time, was the common title of the temporal monarch. And so the glory which was assured to the seed of Abraham was at length concentrated in a Son of David.

The Jewish kingdom was not more stable than the Jewish Theocracy. The first conquests of David were lost. The peaceful sovereignty of Solomon was transitory. Idolatry was established under the shadow of the Temple. But the people had seen the figure of a divine monarchy and never lost what that had taught them. Soon however tyranny, disaster, defeat, captivity, taught them yet more. The spiritual aspect of the bright future to which they looked became more prominent. The great Deliverer was portrayed not only under the guise of the Son of David who should reign for ever in majesty, but also as the servant of GOD, *without form or comeli-* Is. liii. 2, 3. *ness, a man of sorrows and acquainted with grief.* Messiah, the Son of David, was at last regarded as Messiah, the Son of Man.

With this last revelation the inspired prophecies of Messiah the Prophet, the King, the

II. Priest came to an end. Hope, as we see, was gradually concentrated and intensified. Nothing was lost which the past had ever promised, but the sum of all fell infinitely short of that which God was preparing. And then for about four hundred years the Jews were left to ponder over the divine teaching which they had received, unaided by any further voices from heaven. As they listened to the word during that dreary interval the past became more clear to simple and loving hearts; but at the same time it was not so clear that selfishness could not misread it.

We see the end of this discipline of two thousand years in the Gospels. Some there were *just and devout who waited for the consolation of Israel* like Symeon and Anna: some like Nathanael who could yield their prejudices to the influence of a presence recognised as divine: some like St Andrew and St John who could at once follow Him who was made known to them *as the Lamb of* GOD, as the fulfiller of mysterious thoughts stirred by the teaching of sacrifice; some like Martha who in the bitterness of bereavement could still say to Him who had seemed to disregard her prayer: *I have believed*—yea I still believe—*that Thou art the Christ the Son of* GOD *which should come into the world.*

And on the other side there were those who had suffered their own fancies to rise like a cloud between them and the vision of GOD'S love: those

<small>Luke ii. 25, 38.

John i. 46.

John i. 35, 36.

John xi. 27.</small>

who would thrust aside what yet they could not but honour because it did not fall in with their own wishes: those who strove to use by any means that which they felt to be of heaven to work out their own designs: a Herod who could look on Christ as a spectacle: a Caiaphas who could offer Him as a sacrifice for political safety: a Judas who could betray Him, as it seems, to hasten the accomplishment of his selfish ambition.

<small>II.</small>

<small>Luke xxiii. 8.
John xi. 49, 50.
John xiii. 26, 27.</small>

The Gospel of St John from first to last is a record of the conflict between men's thoughts of Christ, and Christ's revelations of Himself. Partial knowledge when it was maintained by selfishness was hardened into unbelief: partial knowledge when it was inspired by love was quickened into Faith.

The Son of Man came to fulfil all the teaching of past history, to illuminate all the teaching of future history; and therefore He first revealed Himself by this title 'Christ' the seal of the fulfilment of the Divine Will through the slow processes of life.

And all this is *written for our learning*. By that title 'Christ,' if we will give heed to it, GOD teaches us to find the true meaning of history: by that title so slowly defined, so variously interpreted, so gloriously fulfilled, He teaches us at all times, and in these times, to wait, to watch, and to hope.

By that title 'Christ' GOD teaches us to

26 *Lessons of waiting,*

II. wait. 'I believe in one Lord Jesus Christ...who shall come again with glory...' That is our profession; but do we attach any real significance to the word? Do we not rather assume that all things will go on as they have gone on for eighteen hundred years? And yet are not these centuries as full of divine warnings, of signs of judgment, of movements towards a kingdom of heaven, as the ages which preceded the first Advent? Without hasting without resting let us move forwards with our faces towards the light to meet the Lord. *In your patience ye shall win your souls:* here is His promise.

Luke xxi. 19.

By that title 'Christ' GOD teaches us to watch. There is the danger now which there was in old time lest we mistake the reflection of our own imaginings for the shape of God's promises. We see a little and forthwith we are tempted to make it all. We yield to the temptation, and become blind to the larger designs of Providence. The cry is ever being raised 'Lo Christ is here' or 'He is there, in the secret chambers, or in the desert'; and if we have indulged in our own self-chosen dreams, we leave the broad fields of life to find our folly end in desolation. Our faith, our wisdom, our safety, lie in keeping ourselves open to every sign of His coming, and then that last lightning flash will reveal to us workings of His about us, influences of His within us, which we could not have been able, could not have dared to recognise before.

Matt. xxiv. 23 ff.

Luke xvii. 24.

For once again by that title 'Christ' GOD teaches us to hope. It is the pledge of His personal love shewn through all the ages. It is the pledge of the final establishment of His kingdom of which the sure foundations are already laid. False hopes, selfish fancies, earthly ambitions were scattered by Christ's first coming. But He brought that into the world which gives their only reality to all the emblems of power. *Thy throne, O God, is for ever and ever: a sceptre of righteousness is the sceptre of Thy kingdom.* Life if we look at it in Christ is transfigured: Death if we look at it in Christ is conquered. When we interpret what He has done through the Church in preparation for His second Coming by the light of what He did through Israel in preparation for His first Coming, we can wait and watch and hope, certain of this in all checks and storms and griefs that He shall *reign till all enemies are put under His feet.*

II.

a Ps. xlv. 6: Hebr. ii. 8.

This and far more than this, which I cannot strive to express, which I cannot hope to understand, lies in that one word 'Christ.' That one word is a historic Gospel hallowing all time. We may grasp but little of its meaning, but if we hold humbly, firmly, lovingly, with a sense of our own great need, what we do know, Christ will reveal Himself to us even as He did aforetime through our imperfect knowledge.

For that is the peculiar teaching of the text.

28 *A revelation to imperfect faith.*

II.
John iii. 2.
John v. 17.
John vi. 15.

Not to the teacher of Israel, not to the disputants at Jerusalem, not to the eager multitudes who offered an army and a throne, but to a simple, sinful woman, an outcast from the synagogue, an alien, the Lord declared Himself to be the Christ. Her expectation was not disturbed by hopes of personal or national aggrandisement. Her difficulties concerned the right approach to GOD. Her faith was imperfect—she knew only what Moses had taught her—but it was sincere. And therefore she found what she felt herself to want and what she was sure GOD had promised.

And so it will be with us. If we can say with honest and true hearts 'I know that Christ when He cometh will illuminate these terrible mysteries of wickedness and suffering which darken the world;' or 'I know that Christ when He cometh will order in one harmonious government all the powers of earth and heaven and man;' or 'I know that Christ when He cometh will lift off my soul the burden of sin by which I am weighed down.' If we can say this, and labour trusting to His Spirit towards the end for which we crave; let us not doubt that to us also, it may be in the noontide heat, when we are weariest, the divine voice will come through some presence which we have misunderstood, bearing in to our soul all the blessings which we have sought and blessings which we could not have imagined, even that voice from the well of Sychar, *I that speak unto thee am He.*

III.

THE BREAD OF LIFE.

I am the bread of life...This is the bread which came down out of heaven: not as the fathers did eat, and died: he that eateth this bread shall live for ever.

St John vi. 35, 58.

I AM the bread of life...This is the bread which came down out of heaven: not as the fathers did eat, and died: he that eateth this bread shall live for ever. These words are the beginning and the close of one of the most mysterious and far-reaching revelations which the Lord has been pleased to make of the relation in which He stands to the world and to believers. The revelation was given at a turning-point in His ministry. It was, we may perhaps say, designed to be what it became, a test of faith. It was received at the time (as it has been received ever since) with questionings, and murmurings, and contentions. Cavillers found in it an excuse for their unbelief. Even disciples found in it an occasion for apostasy. But on the other hand the faithful found in it the assurance of that for which they were looking. And when the question was put to the twelve *Will ye also go away?* the answer was ready *Lord to whom shall we go? Thou hast*

III.

John vi. 67, ff.

III. *words of eternal life, and we have believed and know that Thou art the Holy One of God.*

They are indeed *words of eternal life*. They assure us of the reality of that life: they make known to us the one true support of it; they shew us how we can make that support our own.

This self-revelation of the Lord differs in character from that which we have already considered. When He spoke of Himself as 'the Christ' He declared the relation in which He stands to all history, as fulfilling and interpreting the Divine counsel slowly wrought out on the scene of human discipline. But by this title— 'the Bread of Life,'—as by those which follow, He discloses something of what He is in Himself and for men, special relations in which He stands to believers and to the world, manifold details which go to make up the fulness of the whole life of faith and the harmonious view of His Person. I do not however wish to dwell on this consideration now, which will offer itself more forcibly when we come to review the whole series of titles; but we can see how the series begins naturally with the revelation of life. At the decisive crisis in His work the Lord reveals what life truly is. This is the fundamental conception. He declares that it is through His coming and through fellowship with Him that men can live. He discloses through and in Himself the fact of life, the food by which life is supported, the personal appropriation of the true spiritual food.

The occasion of the revelation. 33

1. *I am the bread of life.* The words sprang directly out of the circumstances under which they were spoken. About the time of the Passover, which perhaps He could not keep at Jerusalem, the Lord had fed five thousand men in the wilderness with five loaves and two small fishes. The multitude with hasty and undisciplined zeal fancied that they saw in this miracle the coming fulfilment of their own wild hopes, and sought to take Jesus by force to make Him a king. When they were foiled in this design, some still followed Him to Capernaum, but only to learn there that they had utterly mistaken the import of Christ's work. *Ye seek Me,* He said, *not because ye saw signs*—not because ye perceived that the satisfying of the hunger of the body was an intelligible parable of the satisfying of the hunger of the soul—*but because ye did eat of the loaves and were filled:* because you looked to me to satisfy mere bodily, earthly, temporal wants: because you brought down the meaning of that one typical work to the level of your own dull souls instead of using it as a help towards loftier efforts: because you still rest in the outward, the sensuous, the transitory, all which I am come to reveal in their true character as symbols, pledges, sacraments of things spiritual and eternal. True it is, such is the general force of the words which follow, if I may venture to paraphrase them, true it is that there is room for your labour even now:

III.

John vi. 4.

John vi. 14, 15.

v. 26.

vv. 28—35.

III. true it is, as you plead, that Moses gave your fathers manna by the word of God not for one meal only, but for forty years in the wilderness. True it is, as you argue, that the greater Moses will give to his people bread from heaven, more copious and more enduring than that perishable food. But while this is so you fatally misunderstand the work, the type, the food. The work—strange paradox—is faith: the type is the faint figure of a celestial pattern: the food is not for the passing relief of a chosen race but for the abiding life of the world. You seek something *from Me* but if you knew the gift of God, you would seek *Me*: *I am the bread of life.*

Such is the connexion in which these divine words stand; and from this point of view we shall see how they help us to rise to the Christian idea of life which Christ lays open through Himself. The old Jewish idea was not wholly cast aside but used to convey new and nobler thoughts. The people were not wrong when they claimed the prerogative of labour: they were not wrong in expecting sustenance from heaven: they were not wrong in looking to the Christ for that which they needed. There is indeed one work in which all separate works are included. There is a divine food which supports that within us which corresponds with itself. The Son of God came that
v. 40. whosoever *believeth on Him may have eternal life.*
Each thought of the Galilean multitude, as we

the expectation of the people.

observe, is thus preserved and raised to a higher and a spiritual region. Life with its struggles, its wants, its inevitable close, is treated as the visible sign of eternal life.

This revelation of Christ as the giver of life meets an inherent want of the human soul.

There is no one of us who does not feel the reality of the higher life when it is thus brought upon him. We know that our multitudinous actions and words cannot rightly be judged by any outward standard; but that there is something in the doing and saying, independent of the mere outward accidents, which gives to them an abiding character. We are conscious within ourselves of some vague looking to and longing for a divine fellowship. We cannot realise death, even when all around reminds us of our mortality. We have powers which find no adequate exercise, desires which find no lasting satisfaction, plans which find no ripe fulfilment. Business and care and pleasure drown the soft voices of the soul which are ever speaking of all these things, but from time to time in those still spaces of silence which come from God, they make themselves heard. At such seasons perhaps we are perplexed by feeling how much that is corruptible is mixed up with our true selves. We compare what we are with what we might have been, with what we aspire to be, and our heart fails us. But

III.

1 John iii. 20.

1 John i. 3.

God is greater than our hearts; and when our doubts are sorest, as Christians we can turn with joy to the thought of our incorporation with Christ. Then we shall know how the divine assurance that we are 'members of Christ' answers the fleeting and yet importunate aspirations which witness within us to an eternal life, to a life beyond time and above it, to a life not future and distant but even now present and active, to a life which includes the possibility of perfect communion with God and man.

2. Eternal life then is a reality, and it is within the reach of each one of us. But this life, of which our earthly sensible life is the veil or the shadow, needs its proper nourishment. It cannot continue apart from that which is its source and its support. The true, living self, like our living bodies, needs for its support that which is of a nature corresponding with it. Man cannot feed on stones, in respect to his outward frame. His body may be built out of the elements which they contain; but he needs that the elements which he appropriates should already have been prepared for him by a vital force. So too it is with his higher life. This also requires sustenance like to itself, and that not in one respect only but in all, covering even now, so far as we can apprehend it, the sum of our human capacities and powers. Spiritual sustenance cannot be effective in an abstract form, as pure Truth: it must come to us through the energy of a spiritual life.

for action and for rest.

The words which immediately follow the first III. announcement of Christ, *I am the bread of life*, shew how this necessity is recognised and met in His teaching. *I am*, He says, *the bread of life:* v. 35. *He that cometh to Me shall never* (in no wise) *hunger, and he that believeth on Me shall never* (in no wise) *thirst.* It is of course quite possible to regard this rich fulness of language as the embellishment of a simple idea, to treat 'coming to Christ,' and 'believing on Christ' as identical; to look on 'hunger' and 'thirst' as mere conventional images of want. But I hardly think that the patient student of St John will be willing to admit that one word of his record fails of its fullest meaning; I hardly think that anyone who has looked into the facts of his own life will feel that one fragment of the promise can be neglected. The apparent repetition meets the necessities of our case. There is an active side to life and there is a passive side. Both are exercised; both are consecrated by our faith. There is need of Christian energy, and effort and movement: there is need also of Christian patience, and rest and waiting. We must *come* to Christ, if we would find in Him our spiritual food; we must leave something in order that we may seek Him; we must use the powers which He has given us in order that we may find Him. And on the other hand we must *believe* in Christ: there is a sense in which our strength must be to stand still: in which our intensest strivings must yet be combined with repose: in which our boldest conflicts must be tempered with a sense of peace in Him. He is at once our remote and future aim, and our immediate and present stay. And His gift corresponds already with this twofold claim. He offers that which will stay our hunger, that which will give strength for labour and restore the waste of the past. And He offers also that which will stay our thirst, that which will bring refreshment after failure and turn our very disappointments into gladness. So it is that man's spiritual food, which is Christ Himself, answers to the varied wants of his higher life; and this it does as being not only a source of life, but also endowed with life. For Christ, as we must notice, uses two phrases in this chapter when He speaks of Himself generally as man's spiritual food. *I am*, He says, *the bread of life;* and yet more than this, *I am the living bread*. I give, that is, what I have inherently: I communicate life because I live. Not by any arbitrary exercise of power, not by any external fiat of omnipotence, but by the impartment of myself, my living self, I sustain the living man. *Because I live*, such is the promise elsewhere, *ye shall live also*. Even in this loftiest region of being, there is no interruption of the supreme unity of the divine law, that life comes from life.

Nor is this all. The bread—the support which

Christ is—is as we have seen *the bread of life*, bringing, that is, the life over which death has no power: it is also *the living bread*, being itself possessed of that life which it conveys: and, yet more, the life which Christ gives, the life which Christ has, is not alien from that of man, but most truly human. It not only satisfies man's wants but answers completely to man's nature. *The bread,* *v.* 51.
He says, Who is Son of Man, *which I will give is my flesh for the life of the world.*

III.

This is the central thought of the whole chapter, and what has been already said will, as I trust, place the revelation in its true light. The *flesh* of Christ is His true Humanity. This He assumed for us; this He gave for us as our complete ransom; this He gives to us as our adequate sustenance. Christ offers us His humanity as the redemption, the support, the transfigurement of our humanity. Through Christ's manhood we are brought into union with Christ, who is God and Man, and in virtue of our fellowship with Him His promise will be fulfilled in us, and He will *raise us up*—such is the four-times repeated burden of the discourse—*He will raise us up* perfect men even as He is perfect man—*in the last day.* *vv.* 39, 40, 44, 54.

3. Thus we are brought to the third point which we have to notice in this revelation of Christ, how it is that this *bread of life*, this *living bread*, this *flesh* of Christ personally avails for each

III.	one of us. One figure is used throughout to de-
v. 50.	clare this mystery. '*I am the bread of life... which cometh down from heaven, that a man may*
v. 51.	*eat thereof and not die.*' '*I am the living bread... if a man eat of this bread he shall live for ever.*'
v. 54.	'*Whoso eateth my flesh and drinketh my blood hath eternal life.*'

Now it is easy to say that 'eating of the bread of life' or 'eating the flesh of Christ,' is a figurative way of describing faith in Christ. But such a method of dealing with the words of Holy Scripture is really to empty them of their divine force. This spiritual eating, this feeding upon Christ, is the last result of faith, the highest energy of faith, but it is not faith itself. To eat is to take that into ourselves which we can assimilate as the support of life. The phrase 'to eat the flesh of Christ' expresses therefore as perhaps no other language could express, the great truth that Christians are made partakers of the human nature of their Lord which is united in One Person to His Divine nature, that He imparts to us now, and that we can receive into our own manhood, something of His manhood, which may be the seed, so to speak, of the glorified bodies in which we shall hereafter behold Him. Faith, if I may so express it, in its more general sense, leaves us outside Christ trusting to Him; but this crowning act of faith incorporates us in Christ: *we abide in Him and He in us.*

John xv. 4.
1 John iii. 24.

the spiritual food.

And when we approach the subject from this side we see the real connexion in which the whole discourse stands with the institution of the Holy Eucharist. It is equally wrong to regard the words as a simple prophecy of that Sacrament, and to dissociate them from it. The words were addressed to the assembly in the synagogue at Capernaum and they are addressed to the Church in all ages. They were spoken so as to be understood at the time, and yet so as to be understood more fully afterwards. They set forth clearly in thought what the Holy Communion presents outwardly in fact. They give the idea of which that gives the pledge.

And here lies the marvel of divine love. Without some such external rite as the Holy Communion we might have doubted as to the fulfilment of the promise of Christ to ourselves. But that at once takes us out of ourselves. That enables us to think only of the Lord, of His words, of His Death, of His Resurrection. We can trust Him wholly. We can believe without reserve what He has said. We can take the bread and wine, broken and blessed according to His commandment, in the sure conviction that through them He gives Himself to us for the strengthening and refreshment of our whole nature. We do not presume to say that Christ gives Himself only in this, but we 'have believed and know' that in this He does give Himself. And then from the Holy Communion we can go forth to our common life, which is shewn to us as all hallowed in that Sacrament, most universal and at the same time most personal, and be assured that Christ will be ever with us: He in us, that we may never despair when we are beset by difficulties, we in Him, that when we have attained something we may reach forward to greater victories.

No words of the preacher can add to the solemnity of this revelation of eternal life and of Christ the food of eternal life, on which I have touched. It has been indeed impossible to do more than touch upon it; but it will be enough if I have encouraged anyone to ponder once again those discourses at Capernaum, which are still, as they were at first, a touchstone of our faith. The chapter is one for prayer and not for controversy. But I do believe that every word will grow luminous if read in the light of heaven. The Spirit will teach us in these later days to understand aright what He brought to the remembrance of St John in his Ephesian exile.

He will teach us to know that beneath all that is poor and fleeting and imperfect in our visible life there is a principle of eternal life by which we, through the infinite grace of God, can claim fellowship with Him. He will teach us that the one only support of this life is Christ Himself, truly God and truly man, who took our

of the revelation. 43

nature and bore our sin that we may be one with Him, and in Him bear the transforming splendour of the open vision of God. He will teach us that the Holy Communion is no strange exceptional service, but in very deed the lively image of our Christian life, and the lively pledge that the fulness of that life is possible for us by participation in Him Who is life. He will teach us by worthier and more sustained resolves, by simpler and tenderer devotion, by more absolute self-forgetfulness, by more vital recognition of Christ's Presence with us and in us, to come to know with more certain assurance and more complete surrender all that lies between the beginning and the end of faith: *I am the bread of life...He that eateth of this bread shall live for ever.*

And while we offer ourselves as humble scholars in His school we shall train our impatient minds to reverent self-restraint. We shall not be hasty to define in forms of human speech truths which pass finally into the unapproachable glory of the Divine Being. We shall confess that we have no powers to determine how things transitory and sensible can become channels of grace eternal and spiritual. Every question even as to earthly life eludes us, if we strive to go beyond the fact and the accompanying circumstances to the cause. Can we wonder that it is so in matters of spiritual life? But where speculation fails, obedience and faith will

III. confirm to us the blessing of Holy Communion, the joy of Holy Eucharist.

So God in His great love will enable us like St Peter to find that these *hard sayings* are to us *words of eternal life.*

IV.

THE LIGHT OF THE WORLD.

I am the light of the world: he that followeth me shall not walk in darkness, but shall have the light of life.

ST JOHN viii. 12.

I AM the light of the world. The Lord gave this revelation of Himself at the Feast of Tabernacles, which was in an especial sense *the Feast of the Jews*, the joyful commemoration of all the blessings of the Exodus, crowned by the occupation of Canaan, the abiding record of that manifestation of the divine Presence which had shaped and inspired their national character. The later history of the chosen people had no doubt fallen far short of the ideal which was offered to them at first for their realisation. The kingdom of Israel had gradually become likened to the kingdoms of the world. Earthly sovereigns had occupied the throne which the Lord had chosen for Himself. A Temple had been substituted for the Tabernacle. An outward system had usurped more and more the place of a living relationship with God. But from year to year the earliest memories of deliverance, of support, of guidance were brought back. Dwelling once

IV.

John vii. 2.

48 *The lessons of the*

IV. again in booths the Jews were forced to think for a time how they were in a past age brought from Egypt and disciplined in the wilderness; how they were still all alike, rich and poor, high and low, citizens in a spiritual commonwealth; how the ingathering of their wealth was coupled with the record of their direct dependence upon Jehovah.

It is not then surprising that the Lord took advantage of this typical Feast to reveal to the multitudes who were gathered at Jerusalem something more of His Person and of His Work than He had made known before. In Him the figures of the Exodus were fulfilled; and it might be that through them the people could be led to know how He satisfied promises to the power of which they themselves were bearing witness at the very time when He addressed them.

Two characteristic ceremonies of this Festival gathered up in expressive symbols the lessons of a divine sustenance and of a divine Presence, which remained as the great results of the teaching of the desert, and both of these were treated by Christ as parables of Himself. Each morning water was brought in a golden vessel from the Pool of Siloam and poured upon the altar of sacrifice. That water recalled to the people the supply drawn from the rock at Meribah, and pointed forward to the spiritual water which
Is. xii. 3. hereafter men should *draw from the well of salvation*. For Christ the living rock, the

image and the prophecy found their accomplishment; and so *in the last day, that great day of the feast, Jesus stood and cried saying If any man thirst, let him come unto Me and drink.* Then again every evening two great lamps were lighted in one of the courts of the Temple which are said to have cast their light over every quarter of the Holy City. These recalled the pillar of fire which had been in old times the sure token of divine leadership and pointed forward to *the sun of righteousness which should rise with healing in His wings.* In Christ—*the light to lighten the Gentiles and the glory of His people Israel*—the image and the prophecy found their accomplishment, and *therefore* He *spake again unto* the people *saying I am the light of the world: he that followeth Me shall not walk in darkness but shall have the light of life.*

IV.
John vii. 37.

Mal. iv. 2.

Luke ii. 32.

This then is the revelation which we have to consider now, for we have already touched upon the revelation of Christ as the support of life; and in order to feel the full significance of the words we must remember their true connexion. For in the original text they follow immediately after the reply of the Pharisees to the pleading of Nicodemus, and so the cavils of the adversaries of Christ are brought into direct contrast with His self-revelation.   The people were wavering and divided: their leaders were blinded by the assumption of infallible knowledge: the dawnings

John vii. 52.

of faith were in danger of being eclipsed by ignorance and prejudice; and at this crisis the Lord breaks through the gathering clouds and calls to Himself all that has fellowship with the light.

I am the light of the world. As we linger over the phrase thoughts of unity, of majesty, of revelation, of insight, of growth, of progress, crowd in upon us. We seem to see how that which had faded away from the eyes of men came back with undying splendour; how that which had been once for the solace and guiding of a single race was given at last for the illumination of mankind: how that which had been but a manifestation of God, was in the fulness of time a personal presence of God, the *Word made flesh and dwelling among us.*

The revelation of Christ as 'the light of the world' follows—we may almost say necessarily—on the revelation of life. Without light, the activity of life is impossible under the conditions of our present existence. Without light, we are unable to apprehend and to distinguish the parts of the general order in which we are placed. Light offers to us a harmony in which the widest diversities are perfectly blended, and by its very presence constrains us to use it thankfully. The creation of light is parallel with the Resurrection and the gift of Pentecost. Earthly light is but a reflection of that which is spiritual.

Light a revelation of beauty.

I am the light of the world. Any one who has watched a sunrise among mountains will know how the light opens out depths of beauty and life where but lately the eye rested on a cold monotony of gloom or mist. At one moment only the sharp dark outline of the distant ranges stands out against the rosy sky, and at the next, peak after peak catches the living fire, which then creeps slowly down their rocky slopes, and woods and streams and meadows and homesteads start out from the dull shadows, and the grass on which we stand sparkles with a thousand dew-drops.   Now all this represents in a figure what is the effect of the Presence of Christ in the world, when the eye is opened to see Him. *All that hath come into being was life in Him,* before time, *and the life was the light of men.* Let the thought of Christ rest on anything about us, great or small, and it will forthwith reflect on the awakened soul some new image of His power and love. Whatever is, was made through Him, and subsists in Him. And it is by the living apprehension of this Truth alone that we can gain any deep insight into the marvels by which we are encompassed.   Thus only can we feel the sanctity, the permanence, nay more, the divinity, of creation underneath that which is fleeting and corruptible and corrupted. Here also the great law is fulfilled that knowledge comes through love, and where the light of Christ rests, there the

IV.

John i. 3, 4.

Col. i. 16, 17.

heart of the believer finds a fulness of teaching which all life is too short to master.

I am the light of the world. The light which reveals the world does not make the darkness, but it makes the darkness felt. If the sun is hidden all is shadow, though we call that shadow only which is contrasted with the sunlight; for the contrast seems to intensify that which is however left just what it was before. And this is what Christ has done by His coming. He stands before the world in perfect purity, and we feel as men could not feel before He came, the imperfection, the impurity of the world. The line of separation is drawn for ever, and the conscience of men acknowledges that it is rightly drawn. Whether we know it or not the light which streams from Christ is ever opening the way to a clearer distinction between good and evil. His coming is a judgment. The light and the darkness are not blended in Him, as they are in us, so that opinion can be doubtful. But His Presence is an absolute revelation of light. In Him we see all that is summed up in the terms self-surrender and self-sacrifice,— all, in a word, that tends to bring man closer to man, and men to God, all that tends to break down the barriers by which we isolate and weaken ourselves,—placed supreme among human virtues. And no darkness can overshadow His luminous Presence.

I am the light of the world. Light has always

The unity and purity of light.

been regarded by the common instinct of men as the emblem of absolute purity, absolute unity. We cannot conceive anything, such is our natural impression, purer or simpler than light. And yet we know that the clear white sunbeam contains in it all the innumerable tints of earth and sky, brought together into one sovereign harmony. We can ourselves break it up at will into the bright colours of the rainbow. And however startling may be the contrasts between the elements when they are seen apart, each element contributes in due measure to the final effect. No single ray however brilliant or however uniform could suggest that idea of infinite fulness which adds a sense of richness to the sense of purity, of life to that of unity. Nothing is more truly one than light yet nothing is more manifold. And surely in this fact we can see faintly portrayed something of the nature of that light which Christ is, and which Christ gives. It includes the sum of every power of man, by which the Being and the Will of God can be known. It is reflected in every object in which we can catch now this now that fragment of the divine brightness. The unity of our faith, the unity of the Church, is like the unity of Christ, the unity of light. Take from it any constituent and the whole will be less pure, less really one than it was before. And if it often happens that we can see nothing but the isolated, coloured, broken gleams, let us remember that this is the very condition of our earthly life. For us the glory of heaven is tempered in a thousand hues, but we know even now that these thousand hues spring from and issue in the light which God is and in which He dwelleth.

1 John i. 5.
1 Tim. vi. 16.

I am the light of the world. Light is self-attested. We do not look for the light doubtfully, or painfully prove its existence. We see it, and we use it. It is vain for the blind man to plead his experience against the experience of all other men. It is no excuse for stumbling or losing our way that we have wilfully closed our eyes. We do not reason with the man who looks heavenward at midday and says that there is no light. Just so it is with Christ. He shines forth upon us in the Gospels, in the life of the Catholic Church, in the life of the individual soul. The light is there and we are not careful to reason about its existence.

There may be some who have no consciousness of clinging, crushing sin which Christ can remove, of evil intruding itself into act and word and thought which He can expel, of gloom overshadowing our life which He can irradiate: some that is who have no feeling for the greatest sorrows and the most glowing hopes of the world. But these cannot set aside the facts to which millions have borne and still bear witness, that sin is a load which Christ can take away, that evil is the work of an enemy of God, whom He came to conquer, and not a necessity of nature, that our Faith opens a prospect far beyond all doubts and temptations in which Love is seen finally triumphant, when God shall be all in all.

There may again be some who in language admit all this, and yet walk with downcast, blinded eyes; as if there were no light to shine along their path; as if it were enough to say 'there is a light' though they do no more. But their failures and follies prove nothing against the power of light to guide, to cheer, to illuminate. If one man only has ever found his life transfigured by Christ in whom he has believed, that is enough. It can be so with us.

Some too there may be, saddest thought perhaps of all, who look upon Christ and see nothing in Him that they *should desire Him*, who seem to find elsewhere what we find in Him, who make the scattered reflections of light springs of light. But hope does not leave us here. It may be that even these ignorantly worship Him whom they affect to deny.

I am the light of the world: he that followeth Me shall not walk in darkness; but shall have the light of life. The light is not given us to gaze at in idle or even in devout wonder, but to lead us forward. We lose the light if we do not follow Christ, and move as He moves. We cannot hold Him back. It is the glory of our faith that it advances with the accumulated progress of all life. And it is our blessing that we are not left to grope sadly and restlessly for our way. That way is a track of light which grows dim only if we loiter or hang back. A Christian cannot rest in anything which has been already gained. New acquisitions of knowledge, new modes of thought, new forms of society, are always calling for interpretation, for recognition, for adjustment. And no one can mistake the problems which the present generation is called to face: no one who has felt in the least degree the power of Christ can doubt that he has in his faith that wherewith to illuminate them. There are the trials of wealth burdened by an inheritance of luxury, which checks the growth of fellow-feeling and enfeebles the energy of Christian love. There are the trials of poverty worn by the struggle for bare existence, which exhausts the forces properly destined to minister to the healthy development of the fulness of life. There is the separation of class from class which seems to become wider with increasing rapidity through the circumstances of modern labour and commerce. There is the concentration of the population in crowded towns where the conditions of dwelling exclude large bodies of men from all share in some of the noblest teachings of nature. There is the exaggerated exten-

Christians are a light.

sion of empires, which brings as its necessary consequence the crushing burden of military expenditure, and at the same time lessens the responsibility of the individual citizen. There is the impatient questioning of old beliefs which gives an unreal value to the appeal to authority and casts suspicion upon sympathetic efforts to meet doubt. But to meet all these dark problems our light—the Light of Life— is unexhausted and inexhaustible. The temple lamps blazed through the early night, but then at last they died out and darkness settled again over the city which lay below. Each borrowed and preparatory light gleamed for a time and afterwards faded away: such lights are consumed in burning. But the Light, which lightens because it lives, which lives (may we not say?) because it lightens, burns on with changeless splendour. And this only is required of us if we would know its quickening, cheering, warming energies, that we should follow it. Only if we 'cling to our first fault,' if we pause when we are called to swift advance, if we faithlessly disbelieve that anything is offered to us, which was not given to those before us, the darkness will overtake us, and our true road will be hidden.

I am the light of the world, so Christ said, and He said also to His disciples *ye are the light of the* Matt. v. 14.

world. The correspondence of the two phrases is most startling, and yet this prerogation of light-bearing is indeed the necessary consequence of discipleship. When Christ ascended from the earth He did not wholly leave it. According to His own promise He is now seen outwardly in those who are His. Each Christian reflects in his measure the light which he receives. Each fulfils, as he may, in the sight of men some fragment of His Lord's office. So we are each constrained to consider with what ministry we are severally charged as *sons of light.*

Christ as the light opens the secrets of the visible order of Nature. We too on our part by reverence, by tenderness, by patience, by watchful and loving care for all creatures can make it felt about us that we look for Him and see Him in His works, and know that through them He is still waiting to teach us more of the wonderful things of His law.

Christ as the light reveals the terrible fact of darkness. And here perhaps our consciences convict us of dissembling too often in daily life the conviction which we feel in our hearts. We smile at evil, we dally with it, we do not confess in act that we hate it with a perfect hatred. And the temptation to this false indifferentism is the more perilous because it comes to us in the guise of humility and self-distrust. It is not then without cause that we are reminded that there are woes in the Gospel: that Christ Himself said *for judgment I came into this world, that they which see not may see, and they which see may become blind.* ^{IV. John ix. 39.}

Christ as the light is the type of unity in manifold cooperation. It is for us then looking to Him to hold what we know in part, as believing that He will complete our partial knowledge through that which He reveals to others. And we may be sure of this that he will ever trust most, hope most, love most, who believes most firmly.

Christ as the light is self-attested. And what dare we say of Christians? Amidst all failures and weaknesses is it not still true that the Christian life, wrought out, as we ourselves must have seen it wrought out, in suffering, in sickness, in poverty, borne and transfigured through the power of the Saviour; wrought out by the use of splendid gifts and high station and large means consecrated and blessed by the love of the Saviour, is the best witness of Christ to those who are without? The age of saints, let us thank God, is not yet past.

Christ as the light sweeps onward to new regions, and thither it is our charge to follow Him. As we look back we can see the course of His Church in a pathway of glory broadening through all the ages. And let us not doubt that the pathway will broaden still. Meanwhile

IV. our part is clear—to look to the Light steadily, to receive the Light heedfully, to spread the Light untiringly. The Light cannot mislead us, and cannot fail us: it is *the Light of Life*.

V.

THE DOOR OF THE SHEEP.

Verily, verily, I say unto you, I am the door of the sheep. I am the door: by me if any man enter in, he shall be saved, and shall go in and go out, and shall find pasture.

ST JOHN x. 7, 9.

THE titles of the Lord which have occupied v.
our attention in the last two lectures present
to us as we have seen, the personal relation in which
He stands to men simply as men. *The bread of* John vi.
God Christ said *is that which cometh down from* 33, 51.
heaven and giveth life not unto a chosen people but
*unto the world...I am the living bread...yea and
the bread which I will give is my flesh, for the life
of the world.* And again *I am the light of the* John viii.
world, the light that is *which lighteth every man.* 12; i. 9.
So far there is nothing peculiar or self-chosen in
the position which we occupy with regard to Him.
The spiritual food is alike for all: the spiritual
light is alike for all. Both may be neglected, but
they are present and adequate to sustain and to
guide mankind. The titles which spring
out of the allegory of the flock to what we come
now, introduce us to a new succession of thoughts.
Christ as *the door* and as *the good shepherd* is
revealed to us as standing in a special connexion

v. with a definite body committed to His protection and care. These titles teach us that there are those who are gathered into His fold: those whom He rescues from dangerous enemies: those whom He leads in green pastures. It is not indeed the exclusiveness but the reality of the privilege suggested by these figures which is set before us. Such figures help us to feel that as Christians we are socially and individually brought very near to Christ, and that He fulfils for us offices of watchful and tender love. And thus their general scope is clearly indicated by the circumstances under which they were first employed. By the sign at
John ix. the Pool of Siloam Christ had vindicated His claim to be the light of the world. It was in vain that the Pharisees tried to persuade the man born blind who had received sight from Jesus that he owed nothing to his healer. To him the work itself was a luminous witness of a divine mission, and he held to this confession even at the cost of being expelled from the Jewish body by the rulers
John ix. 35, 36. who mocked him. So when *Jesus heard that they had cast him out, He found him* and made Himself known to him as *the Son of Man*, and received the homage of his simple faith. Here then was the first clear antagonism between the old church and the new, the first sharp division between the blind guides and the people whom they misled: the first reception into Christ's fellowship of one who had been rejected by the

the Door and the Good Shepherd are revealed. 65

Jews: the first open fulfilment of Christ coming for judgment *that those who saw not might see, and those who saw might become blind.*

<small>V.
John ix. 39.</small>

It was not therefore surprising that *those of the Pharisees which were with Jesus...said unto Him Are we blind also?* The question was answered by a short stern sentence, and by a living picture, for we must bring the tenth chapter into close connexion with the ninth. *Jesus said unto them If ye were blind ye should have no sin: but now ye say We see; therefore your sin remaineth.* And then we may suppose that He turned His eyes to the hillside of Olivet where the shepherds were busy, as evening drew on, with the folding of their flocks, and pointed to the image of spiritual ministry and spiritual relationships in their familiar labour.   It is, as if He had said, 'These shep-
'herds before us, these humble servants of weak
'and wandering creatures shall be your judges.
'You see the fold: how do they enter it? you
'see the flock: how do they treat it? *They* do not
'choose at will a way into the fold which may
'seem best or easiest to themselves, but pass with
'their sheep through the one door however low or
'narrow or ill-placed it may seem to be. *They* do
'not regard their sheep as strangers, but call them
'by name, and go before them, and so receive from
'them trustful obedience. How then have you
'dealt with the sacred enclosure of the Church of
'God? How have you dealt with the flock of

<small>John ix. 40, 41.</small>

66   *Two thoughts: the fold, the flock.*

V.   'God which He entrusted to your keeping and
'guidance?'

Such is the general scope of the whole allegory.
But the words fell on dull ears. The sense of
duty, of devotion, of sacrifice which alone could
make them intelligible was wanting; and the
John x. 6. Pharisees—the shepherds of Israel—*understood
not what things they were which* Jesus *spake to
them.* Yet once again therefore Christ drew out
more in detail the lesson which He wished to bring
home to them and to all, separating the two chief
elements in it which had before been left undis-
tinguished. For we must notice that in the
allegory there are two distinct images, the image
of the fold and the image of the flock. The fold
must be entered: the flock must be kept. The
thought of the entrance comes first: the thought
of the tending follows. It is with regard to the
former that Christ says *I am the door,* just as He
says afterwards with reference to His pastoral care
I am the good shepherd. In these two respects He
condemns the false leaders, and the false teachers:
they were on the one side *thieves and robbers* and
on the other *hirelings.*   It is the former aspect
of the allegory which presents Christ as the Door
that we have to consider now. For if we wish to
enter into the fulness of the revelation which Christ
gives, we must keep the thoughts apart; we must
dwell on each relation separately if we are to make
it a reality and not have it a mere indistinct figure.

Christ the Door of the sheep.

I am the door of the sheep, I am the appointed way, that is, by which all believers, teachers and taught alike, enter into a place of security, of freedom, of nourishment; as it is expressed more fully in the later verse: *I am the door: by Me if any man enter in he shall be saved, and shall go in and go out, and shall find pasture.* These then are the ideas of which we must take account in order to understand the words of the Lord, first the idea of a fold in itself, of some outward enclosure, so to speak, into which we gain entrance only through Christ, and still beyond this the ideas of security, of wide liberty, or rich abundance which Christ gives to those who have been brought within His fold. For the Door is not for use once only, that we may gain admittance into safe precincts and then lie down in idle peace, but for that daily going out and coming in which sums up the activity, the influence, the growth of the Christian: it is regarded primarily in connexion with life and not with order. Christ reveals Himself specifically as the Door of the sheep and not as the Door of the fold.

And here it may be observed that, even if we suppose that this image of the door in its first application, as in its origin, must be referred to those on whom the charge of a pastoral office is laid, still it has also a clear meaning for all Christians, of which alone I shall speak. The position of the pastor, so far as we are concerned with it now, passes directly into that of the believer.

We may then proceed to develop the thoughts which I have indicated in this their most general aspect. And it will strike us immediately that the idea of a fold, of a religious society marked by a definite organisation, sharply separated from all around, which was the life of Judaism, the life of the mediæval Church, has grown somewhat alien from our common modes of thinking at the present time. Various causes have contributed to deprive the idea of that external simplicity which it once had. The manifold offices of life have become deeply complicated; the Christian Body has been grievously torn and divided; there is a popular notion that we can in some way secure the spirit of faith without the form of faith. It was easy to look upon the Church of Christ, as indeed a fold in the midst of the world, when outward signs of the truth were everywhere offered to men's eyes, when the great monastery, for example, of which this Cathedral is but a fragment, rose as a place of refuge between the fens and the moorlands, securely fenced against the attacks of pirates and robbers; but it is not easy now. And yet the idea is a true one: it belongs to the essence of Christianity as answering to the fulness of our human nature: it is consecrated for us in the Sacraments. And we lose very much by not practically realising it. For so it comes to pass that the sense of fellowship, of coöperation, of strength is diminished among us: that the spirit of obedience, of loyalty, of reverence is weakened: that the constraining power of the noble memories of a great and enduring society is impoverished. The privileges of outward communion with the Christian Body may have been exaggerated and misrepresented, but they are not visionary. Such communion is a cause for devotion and not for arrogance; an opportunity for effort and not an excuse for indolence. The knowledge that we have been admitted into Christ's fold, through Christ in His own appointed way, enables us to place our confidence in Him and not in ourselves, in an outward fact and not in any fleeting and variable impression. *We* may fail, but He cannot deny Himself. He has received us under His shelter, and if we look to Him He will teach us to use in some new way, suited to our present wants, all that we have inherited from our forefathers of the organisation of the visible Church.

This then is the first point: we have been brought through Christ *the Door* into His Fold, which is not a mere figure of speech but a reality. In virtue of this reception by Him we occupy a position of security. *I am the door: by Me if any man enter in he shall be saved.* We are of course warned by other passages of Holy Scripture from extending this description of the present state and privileges of Christians to their final condition. What is chiefly brought before us is that man's place in natural society is one of great danger: that he is exposed on all sides to influences and temptations which may work his ruin: that there are objects of attraction which he must abandon. Now if the idea of the visible Church has grown vague among us, the idea of that which is called 'the world' in the New Testament has grown even more vague. No doubt presumptuous teachers have erred in attempting to define the world as opposed to the Christian society too precisely in detail; but no one can read the apostolic writings without feeling that the contrast between the two is that of irreconcileable opposites, which it concerns us vitally to apprehend. There is a kingdom of the world, a prince of the world, a friendship of the world, an invisible organisation of the powers of the world. Such truths give a mysterious and intense solemnity to our human existence; but not to dwell on these at present, we may say simply that life in and of the world is directed (as we know life may be directed) to that which is finite, transitory, sensuous, selfish; that the course of such a life is antagonism to God; and that its end is death. From this antagonism, from this death, Christ saves us. Life entered on through Him, life in Him is directed to that which is infinite, eternal, spiritual, divine. And without going one step further we can see how *new relations with God and man.* 71

this essential difference of the two forms of life
offered to us marks the character of the great
conflict in which we must take part as men poised
between heaven and earth; we can see that the
dangers of 'the world' are inevitable and inherent
in finite beings; we can see that they are not
conjured up by the imagination of formalists since
they lie in the constitution of our own nature: we
can see that by passing through Christ—through
Him who became incarnate and lived and died
and rose again for us—into new relations with one
another and with God, we do indeed enter on a
state of safety, in which every fragment of life is
consecrated, and therefore stamped with the
divine signs of sacrifice and permanence.

But the fold which the Christian enters through
Christ, the fold which gives safety to the flock,
is a place for shelter and not a place for isolation.
He who has passed into it and found in it his
proper home, finds it also a vantage ground for
wider action. When the time comes he passes
out, but he still observes this law, that he passes
out through Christ. *I am the door, by Me if any
man enter in he...shall go in and go out and shall
find pasture.* The Christian indeed alone,
in virtue of his belief in Christ, both God and
man, can feel the true glory of the world, which as
the work of God through the Word is still the
object of the love of God and a revelation of the
Word. If the world on the one side stands apart

from God and alienated from Him, and so doomed to corruption, it is on the other side capable of reunion with Him. Therefore it is that the Christian goes forth, as His Lord opens the way, to claim fresh victories for the Faith, to quicken in others the sense of the unseen behind the seen, to set forth the eternal which underlies things temporal. And as he does so, as he bears this Gospel to the world, as he calls men to recognise that for which they are restlessly seeking, as he interprets voices of the Word in the Life which subsists in Him, as he reveals the dimmed glories of *the Light which lighteth every man* struggling through the darkness, so he himself *finds pasture*. The fold offers no safety to those who climb over into it by some arbitrary way; and on the other hand the world is a barren wilderness only for those who do not approach it through Christ. But for those who do so approach it, for those who look upon all creation and all life through Him, regarding it as He has made it known, even the world is a garden of the Lord, in which they may find all they need for their refreshment and support. It is the characteristic of the false teacher that *he comes to steal and to kill and to destroy:* he seeks to use those who trust in him for his own ends, to abridge the range of their affections and powers, to narrow the field of their interests; but Christ said of believers *I came that they may have life and may have abundance.*

The Christian then passes into the world, doing His Master's work there, by the way which His Master opens, but he does not remain in the world. He never wanders so far, he never is so deeply engrossed in the pursuits to which he is guided, as not to return to the fold when the darkness falls and the time of working is over. He never forgets that he is one of a definite body fenced by peculiar safeguards, bound by paramount obligations, participating in common privileges. This consciousness of outward union with his fellows is never lost in the acknowledged variety of service. When his task is accomplished he enters again by the narrow and living Door into those closer conditions of communion which supply him with confidence, with strength, with safety, with the energies of inspiring sympathy, with the resources of eternal life.

I am the door : by Me if any man enter in, he shall be saved, and shall go in and go out, and shall find pasture. The words speak to us, as we have seen, of a sacred society into which we are gathered by Christ Himself: they speak to us of outward duties and outward blessings to which we pass through Him: they speak to us of safety, while we remain under His shelter, from the perils and foes by which we are surrounded: they speak to us of a ceaseless conflict waged through Him to recover realms which an enemy has occupied in part: they speak to us of spiritual food which we can win as He reveals Himself to us in our common work: they speak to us of union visibly presented in our life of which He is the Keeper.

May God grant to us to listen to these lessons of privilege in which we all share, of duty to which we are all called, of fellowship to which we are all pledged, and day by day to realise them more perfectly in our lives.

VI.

THE GOOD SHEPHERD.

I am the good shepherd: the good shepherd layeth down his life for the sheep.

I am the good shepherd; and I know mine own, and mine own know Me, even as the Father knoweth Me, and I know the Father.

St John x. 11, 14.

IN speaking in the last lecture of the general scope of the allegory of the Shepherd and the Flock, I endeavoured to shew that it contains two distinct thoughts which are separated by the Lord in the application which He makes of it to Himself, that of the Fold and that of the Flock. Christ is the Door; and He is the Shepherd. The first image presents to us the common relation in which He stands to Christians in virtue of His own Nature, and, answering to this, their position as members of His visible Church. The second image presents to us the closer view of His personal care at once for the whole Flock, and also for the individual members of which it is composed.

We have seen that through Christ as the Door we gain entrance into a state of safety, in which all the elements of our nature are consecrated and so made capable of eternal life: that through Him we go out into the world and find pasture there, because He reveals Himself to us under things temporal wherein others vainly seek satisfaction and find death: that through Him we return to the Fold when the evening falls and our day's work is done, that so we may renew our strength and faith by the sense of fellowship and security to which He alone opens the living way.

Leaving these thoughts then, as already familiar, we pass on to the consideration of the second image of the allegory, Christ as the Good Shepherd. And of all the images of Christ this is that which has ever appealed most forcibly to the universal instincts of men. It has been illustrated by art: it has been consecrated by history. When believers first sought to write the symbols of their faith upon the walls of the catacombs they drew Christ as a Shepherd. And that earliest figure has never passed away from us. Many who care little for painting must have hung with affection over the picture in which the Saviour is shewn patiently and lovingly disentangling the lamb from the thorns by which it is imprisoned and torn. Many who care little for music must have been soothed by the air in which the office of Messiah the Shepherd has been described in universal language. All that we can imagine of tenderness, of endurance, of courage, of watchfulness, of devotion is gathered up in the thought of the pastoral charge; and that charge Christ has taken over us.

From the earliest times men have felt the beauty and the truth of the image.   VI.

The oldest of Greek poets speaks of kings as 'shepherds of men,' but for the Jews this aspect of authority was set forth by living parables in each great crisis of their national growth. The patriarchs were shepherds: Moses was a shepherd: David was a shepherd. When the prophet pictured defeat to Ahab he said: *I saw all Israel scattered* *upon the hills as sheep that have not a shepherd.* 1 Kings xxii. 17. In the Exile Ezekiel cried *Woe be to the shepherds* *of Israel that do feed themselves! should not the* *shepherds feed the flocks?* And this was his great promise of hope to the people restored and purified: *they all shall have one shepherd.* The transition of thought from the earthly ruler to the heavenly was natural and even necessary; and David gathered up his experience on the hill sides and upon the throne in the memorable confession which lives through all time and beyond time: *The Lord* *is my shepherd.* Ezek. xxxiv. 2 ff.

id. xxxvii. 24.

Ps. xxiii. 1.

It is easy to see how these varied memories gathered round the words of Christ, and gave them an intenser meaning; but the prayer which Moses offered in the prospect of his own death is, as it were, a literal prophecy of Messiah's work *Let the* LORD, *the God of the spirits of all flesh,* *set a man over the congregation, which may go out* *before them, and which may go in before them, and* *which may lead them out, and which may bring* Num. xxvii. 15.

80 *Two aspects of the Shepherd's office,*

VI.   them *in; that the congregation of the* LORD *be not as sheep which have no shepherd.* Partial and passing fulfilments of the petition there were in earlier times; and then at last the visions of patriarch, and lawgiver, and king, and prophet found their accomplishment in the Son of man; and so He said in the presence of the disciples who followed His steps with faithful yet wondering devotion, of the Pharisees who darkened the truth which had been committed to their keeping, of the outcast whom the popular leaders had driven
Hebr. xiii. 20.   from their fellowship, *I am the good shepherd,* not *the great shepherd* only, from the wide exercise of authority, or *the true shepherd* only, from the complete satisfaction of the idea, but *the Good Shepherd, good* in the winning beauty of His person and His work which men can see, *good* in the infinite grace shadowed forth by a ministry of love.

Out of the manifold traits of the pastoral character two are selected by the Lord to define the nature of His own pastoral office, as it is seen without in its fulfilment, and as it exists within in its essential foundation. *I am the good shepherd: the good shepherd giveth His life for the sheep.* There is a complete devotion to the charge which issues in absolute sacrifice of self: that is the outward standard of the shepherd's duty. *I am the good shepherd, and know my sheep and am known of mine.* There is an

devotion and sympathy.

underlying sympathy between the leader and the flock which issues in a perfect communion of affection: that is the law of the Shepherd's life.

These two thoughts then claim our separate attention.

I am the good shepherd: the good shepherd giveth his life for the sheep. When the Lord spoke the words He alone could foresee their literal fulfilment, but His disciples must have already learnt to feel that His tenderness was stronger than death. They might say of shame and of suffering 'Far be it from Thee', but they knew at least that, if need were, He would meet both for their sakes. They had found a new kind of discipleship in which the Master lived for His scholars, and not the scholars for the master; in which the relation was not one of contract but of nature, in which dangers were to be expected, but these not greater than love could overcome. Christ the Good Shepherd transfigured for ever the method, the conception, the fulfilment of leadership.

Nothing could be more foreign to the customs of the time than the way in which Christ gathered His little company. He was not like one of the great doctors far withdrawn from common eyes, sought out painfully by those whom His fame had reached, scantily dispensing His wisdom to such as were admitted to His presence. He Himself *found* those who would not have

John ix. 35.

dared to come to Him, who could hardly have interpreted their own wants, who were conscious perhaps only of their need of guidance. With a word of power He called the fisherman and the toll-gatherer to follow His steps. Sinners who hated their sin were welcomed to His fellowship. A band of women ministered to Him. He came to seek and to save, not to receive the homage of the proud or to increase the treasures of the affluent. He presented Himself in a word as the shepherd whose sheep had strayed.

For in the next place the image set before the hearers this thought, that though they had wandered they still belonged to Christ: that He had come to restore, to exalt, to perfect, a connexion which existed, and not to establish a new one: that in this lay the infinite difference between the shepherd, and *the hireling whose own the sheep are not*. The hireling takes upon him, so to speak, something to which he is not born, and which he can lay aside; but the shepherd only shews what he is by his care. The hireling is moved by self-interest, the shepherd by self-sacrifice. In the one case there is a mercenary bargain for the performance of certain definite duties, which is external, artificial, liable to be disturbed or broken by a thousand causes; but in the other case there is simple obedience to an instinct which is inherent and vital. That which belongs to a man, is, as it were, a part of himself. It is *the hireling.*

unnatural, and not simply dishonourable in any one not to cherish and tend and guard that which is his own. And Christ was pleased so to portray His relation to men, as if He were constrained by some divine necessity of nature to fulfil for them a shepherd's work.

At the same time He warned His disciples that they could not be exempt from alarms and perils, even while He watched over them. With the darkness, it might be, the wolf would come. Yet in this last extremity they could trust Him in whose guardianship they had reposed. If nothing else remained He could lay down His life for them. It might not appear obvious how the death of the shepherd could secure the safety of the flock: that was a mystery at the time and is so even now when we look back upon the accomplished fact: but this much at least faith could dimly see, that such devotion could not be in vain, and through that assurance believers could hold themselves prepared for the worst assaults of evil.

This thought brings us to the second point. The care of the Good Shepherd rested upon a divine knowledge. Christ reminded His disciples that this His promise of watching even unto death was only the visible expression of a fellowship of which they were already conscious: *I am the good shepherd*, he said, *and know my sheep and am known of mine.* There may be sad confusions, and rivalries, and antagonisms, and schisms, but through the din and tumult of the world Christ *calleth his own sheep by name* and *they know his voice.* In that mutual knowledge, in that voice of grace answered by the effort of obedience, lies the certainty of hope. Christ knows His own, and as He knows them He imparts to them a unity with Himself. His own know Christ and as they know Him, they appropriate fresh measures of His strength. Christ the Good Shepherd revealed the law of leadership in the gradual realisation of boundless sympathy. There is an infinite spring of consolation in the conviction that Christ knows His disciples: that He knows them, and loves them still. If it were otherwise, if He knew them only as their friends know them, only as they know themselves with a partial and imperfect memory, there might still be room for endless misgivings. The fear would remain lest some fresh revelation might turn His tenderness into sorrow. But as it is nothing in His flock is hidden from Him: their weaknesses, their failures, their temptations, their sins: the good which they have neglected when it was within reach: the evil which they have pursued when it lay afar: all is open before His eyes. He knows them, as I said, and He loves them still.

And in their turn they know Him. Experience has taught them something of the gentleness

A divine foundation.

with which He supports and guides their faltering steps, something of the sweet sternness with which He calls them back from wandering, something of the beneficence with which He opens fresh pastures to them in the way of their common duties, something of the calm peace which He gives as the end of labour which has brought no other reward, something of the joy which He instils into those who are made worthy to follow Him most closely. A thousand strange voices may address them with more immediate and imperious commands; but His voice is clear among them all, and their true selves obey that only: *a stranger will they not follow, for they know not the voice of strangers.*

But wonderful as this second revelation of the Good Shepherd is as we commonly read it, the true connexion in the original text gives it a more mysterious solemnity: *I am the good shepherd; and I know mine own and mine own know Me, even as the Father knoweth Me, and I know the Father.* The relation of the Father to the Son is thus made the type of the relation of the Son to His disciples. We can indeed penetrate as yet but a little way into the meaning of such words; but they help us to feel by the manner of devout thankfulness rather than of distinct apprehension that we too are partakers of the divine nature, that the Son of Man in His humanity has revealed to us the end to which we are called, the victory which he has made possible as being an essential part of the will of God.

So it is that the blessing of the words comes unchanged, as God is unchangeable, even unto us. For every lesson, every promise, which they conveyed to the first disciples, they convey to us now confirmed, extended, deepened by all that our fathers have told us of their manifold fulfilments.

Christ the Good Shepherd has, we know, laid down His life for us, and in His Cross He has given us the measure of the love by which He will draw all men unto Him.

John xii. 32.

Christ the Good Shepherd calls us by name, in every holy thought, in every public service, in every occasion for sacrifice, and as long as the call is audible, we may be sure that He will give the power to obey its leading.

Nor can we forget that by consecrating this figure as the image of His power, Christ has given us a revelation of the character of all true government. While He tells us what He is to us, He tells us what we should strive to be to others. That which He makes known of His relation to His people is true of all right exercise of authority. It does not matter whether authority be exercised in the Church, or in the nation, or in the city, or in the factory, or in the school, or in the family: the two great principles by which it must be directed are the same; and these are self-sacrifice and sympathy. Government which rests on any other basis is so far a tyranny and no true government. We claim then in Christ's name, we can claim no less, that whoever is called to rule, to be priest or statesman or teacher or master should be prepared to give His life for His own, to know them himself, and to be known by them.

Perhaps the most urgent perils of our age spring from the forgetfulness of this divine theory of government. There is much of the spirit of the hireling among us: there is more of the affectation of the spirit. We hide ourselves, and we make but little effort to penetrate to the hearts of others. The nobility of leadership has been degraded in conception, if not in act. The transitory accessories of popularity and wealth and splendour have obscured that absolute devotion to others which is its life. It has been supposed to end in lofty isolation and not in the most intense fellowship. But with all this, there are among us nobler strivings after a truer and more abiding order: there is an impatience of the unnatural ignorance by which we are separated from one another as classes and as individuals: there are generous impulses which move men with aspirations towards silent yet complete self-surrender: there is something of an awakened capacity to embody in the nation and in society the central truths of the gospel. Here as it seems lies the work of England in this generation; and while our thoughts are turned to the Good Shepherd, may we pray for ourselves and for others that He will infuse the virtue of His Life and Passion into each office which we have to discharge for our families, for our country, for our Church; that He will lay the print of His Cross upon all the symbols of our power, and enlighten our counsels with the insight of His Love.

VII.

THE RESURRECTION AND THE LIFE.

I am the resurrection and the life: he that believeth on Me, though he die, yet shall he live; and whosoever liveth and believeth on Me shall never die.

St John xi. 25, 26.

WE read at the end of St John's record of the first miracle of Christ at Cana of Galilee, that thereby He *manifested His glory and His disciples believed in Him*. In other words that *beginning of signs* was a divine revelation. Faith was the essential condition of understanding it; and faith found in it support and growth. The same law is observed in the close of Christ's signs, which St John has preserved, the raising of Lazarus at Bethany; and, as we might have expected, it is illustrated in the details of this crowning act of love and power with fuller light. So it is that the raising of Lazarus was accomplished as a manifestation of the glory of God in Christ: it was a last message to the world, presenting in a figure the lively portraiture of Christ's work. The fact itself encompassed with every circumstance of pathos, and tenderness and majesty, quickened in the minds of those who witnessed it devotion, as it might be, or faith, or

VII.

John ii. 11.

John xi. 40.

The raising of Lazarus

fear, according as they were predisposed to regard it; but we feel that the fact was also in a true sense a ⁓sacrament, an outward pledge of a spiritual grace with which humanity was enriched for ever. If, as indeed we are bound to do, we strive to set before ourselves with vivid particularity the various emotions which are crowded into the narrative, the bitter regret for help unbrought, the sudden awakening of vague hope, the mysterious grief of the Lord Himself, the awful suspense before the opened cave, it must be that we may the better realise that Truth which calms and satisfies them all. The miracle is nothing more than the translation of an eternal lesson into an outward and intelligible form. The command of sovereign power *Lazarus come forth* is but one partial and transitory fulfilment of the absolute and unchanging gospel *I am the resurrection and the life*.

I am the resurrection and the life. In these words, as we have seen before in the like phrases, Christ turns the thoughts of His hearers from all else upon Himself. The point at issue is not any gift which He can bestow, not any blessing which He can procure, but the right perception of what He is. The Galilæans asked Him for the bread from heaven; He replied *I am the bread of life*. The people were distracted by doubt: their leaders were blinded by prejudice; and He said *I am the light of the world*. Martha after touching

John vi. 48.

John viii. 12.

with sad yet faithful resignation upon aid apparently withheld, fixed her hope on some remote time, when her brother should rise again at the last day; and He called her to a present and personal joy. He revealed to her that death even in its apparent triumph wins no true victory: that life is something inexpressibly vast and mysterious, centred in one who neither knows nor can know any change, that beyond the earth-born clouds, which mar and hide it, there is an infinite glory of heaven in which men are made partakers. This revelation Christ makes with absolute knowledge of all human needs. He alone could feel to the uttermost the intensity of the grief which He came to stay: He alone could discern the spring of all sorrow in the sin which He came to bear: He alone could foresee that the immediate issue of His work of sovereign power would be His own death upon the Cross: and yet looking full upon the desolation which seemed to plead against the truth of the words, full upon the infirmity and guilt of men which seemed to make their application impossible, full upon the Agony and Passion which seemed to disprove them, He said *I am the resurrection and the life:* not 'I shall be,' but *I am,* even in the crisis of bereavement, even in the prospect of the Cross; not *the Resurrection* only, but *the Life,* that permanent and eternal power of which it is one result, but only one result, that men shall rise again.

There are thus two main thoughts in this revelation of Christ which we must notice. It teaches us, as I have already indicated, that the Resurrection and the Life in which we believe are realities which are not future only but present: it teaches us also that both lie in our union with a Person. Our faith, in the last trial to which it must be subjected, reaches out beyond the seen, and aspires to a fulness of being which transcends all experience.

I am the resurrection and the life : he that believeth in Me though he die yet shall he live; and whosoever liveth and believeth on Me shall never die. Christ, in a word, is the Resurrection of the dead : Christ is the life of the living: He is the Resurrection because He is the Life. Death is the dream, the shadow ; and not life, as we hastily judge who measure being by our senses.

This then is the first point. Life, eternal life, and therefore the Resurrection, as included in it, is brought to men by Christ now. Christ shews by His word, and by the speaking fact of the recall of Lazarus to earthly life, that what we see is but a small part of what we are, that physical death touches only the circumstances of our present existence, that dissolution is the condition of a new form of life but not an interruption, still less the close, of life. And if we study the whole narrative carefully we shall perceive that from first to last this history of the raising of

Lazarus is a revelation of death and life: a help VII.
given to us through which we may, however
imperfectly and momentarily yet truly, rise to a
better understanding of the nature of our manhood,
than the common experience of the visible world
can furnish. It seems to say that life in its
fulness flows from what men call death, and death
from what men call life. When Christ first heard
of the sickness of Lazarus, though He knew the
speedy issue, He said *This sickness is not unto* John xi. 4.
death. When the worst was over, He called death
a sleep only: *Our friend Lazarus sleepeth, but I go* v. 11.
that I may wake him out of sleep. When Thomas
could see but one end to the mission of love and
said in hopeless devotion *Let us also go that we* v. 16.
may die with Him, he knew not that this journey
of the Lord into the camp of His enemies should
lay open as the disciples had not seen them before,
the very springs of life, though in another sense
it was the way to death. In this relation
there is a tragic eloquence in the opening and the
close of the narrative. It opens on the scene of
John's witness beyond Jordan: it closes in the
council chamber at Jerusalem. The testimony of
the Baptist is repeated involuntarily by the High
Priest. The mysterious words *Behold the Lamb* John i. 29.
of God which taketh away—taketh away by
taking upon Himself—*the sin of the world,* find
their accomplishment in the calculated sentence John xi.
It is expedient for us that one man should die for 50.

the people and that the whole nation perish not. Caiaphas thought to save the life of the Jews by the death of Christ, while in reality by gaining his object he brought death to that false and selfish life, and life to the world.

Thus by every detail of the history we are encouraged to look below the surface of things, to realise how life, true life, triumphs over death and even through death; to regard the restoration of Lazarus not as a mere marvel only but as a type of the constant action of God who preserves through every vicissitude all that which makes us what we are; to know by that staying of the power of corruption, by that call to renewed activity, that Christ as He is the Food to support us, the Light to guide us, is also the Life—infinite and eternal—by which we live.

So we come to the second chief thought suggested by the words: *I am the resurrection and the life.* The Resurrection and the Life is not simply through Christ but in Christ. *I am* He said, and not I promise, or I bring, or I accomplish, *I am the resurrection and the life.* And when we fix our attention upon the words from this point of sight, we see at once that they include deeper mysteries than we can at present fathom, that they open out glimpses of some more sublime form of being than we can at present apprehend, that they gather up in one final utterance to the world what had been said before darkly and partially of the union of the believer with his Lord and of the consequences which proceed from it.

But though we can perhaps do no more, it is well that we should at least devoutly recognise that we do stand here in the face of a great mystery, which if indistinct from excess of glory, yet even now ennobles, consecrates, transfigures life: which does even now help us to feel where is the answer to difficulties which our own age has first been called to meet: which gives a vital reality to much of the language of Holy Scripture which we are tempted to treat as simply metaphorical.

I am the resurrection and the life. The words carry us back to what St John said of the Word in the opening verses of the Gospel: *That which hath been made was life in Him.* It is no doubt very hard for us to think of this divine life underlying all that we see around us in endless change and motion, imperfect, inconstant, conflicting; and still the life is there, and that life is Christ. Man is in a true sense according to the expressive language of old thinkers, a Microcosm, a miniature universe, and he cannot with impunity dissociate himself from the great universe of which he is the representative and the crown. The thought is one which belongs to the very essence of our faith, and we are taught by the Lord's words to cherish it. We cannot with our present faculties pursue it far; but is it not a joy to feel

John i. 3 f.

that this vast life, this life of the whole world carries with it the assurance of a resurrection, of a *restoration of all things*, for which creation *travaileth until now, waiting for the manifestation of the sons of God?*

We commonly lose much, I believe, by neglecting this widest relationship of man with the world, which the Scriptures, anticipating the latest physical theories, affirm on its divine side. We lose even more by neglecting the relationship of man with man. However much we may strive to keep ourselves alone, to narrow our wants, to strengthen our self-reliance, we are driven by the least reflection to acknowledge that we are bound one to another, that we are bound to the past, that we are brethren united by an indissoluble kinsmanship, children with an ineffaceable heritage, that our separate lives are but fragments of some larger life, and that life again is Christ's. He quickens us not as individual units, but as parts of Himself: He raises us up not to stand alone, but as members of His glorified Body. He trains us while we are still kept apart from one another by the conditions of mortality to reach forward to this loftier fellowship; He communicates to us His flesh, His humanity, in which is the fulness of union; He warns us that selfishness, isolation, is death.

This being so, we come to understand, so far as man can understand such teaching, what St

Paul means when he speaks of the Christian as being *in Christ, living in Christ, speaking in Christ, sanctified in Christ*: when he transfers to the individual believer all the acts of Christ: when he argues that he himself died with Christ and was raised again with Christ: when he pleads that we are *one body in Christ*. For all this is but a writing out at length of the Lord's own words, *I am the resurrection and the life*. Whatever life man has, it is in fellowship with Christ, wherein there is already made a beginning of that supreme life of which the life of the family, of the nation, of the Church, of the race, are so many types and foreshadowings.

VII.
1 Cor. i. 30;
Gal. iii. 28;
2 Cor. ii.
17; 1 Cor.
i. 2; 2 Tim.
iii. 12.

Rom. xii.
5; vi. 8 ff.

But while we look forward to the completed revelation of this larger life in which we shall each in due proportion consciously contribute to the fulness of a being of which we are made partakers, we know at the same time that nothing will be lost which belongs to the perfection of our present being. When Christ told His disciples of the death of Lazarus, He added to the name the one title which expressed all that Lazarus had been, all that he still was, to them: *Our friend Lazarus sleepeth*. When He brought relief to Martha, He repeated the word in which she had summed up the extent of her bereavement: *Thy brother shall rise again*. How it is that the fruits of affection and kinsmanship can be taken up into and harmonised with a new form of

John xi.
11.

v. 23.

existence we cannot tell. It is vain for us, nay far worse than vain, to seek to transfer directly to another order the limitations, the modes of action and dependence, which belong to this in which we now are. It is enough for us that, as Christ's words assure us, human ties have a living permanence in Him: that they survive the transitory sphere in which they have here found their growth: that they await a resurrection in which they shall be seen in their true glory. And therefore it is that when we bear to their last resting-place those whom we have loved these words first greet us at the churchyard gate with the certain promise that our love is not lost: therefore it is that we can humbly trust that when they shall be addressed hereafter to friends who shall carry us forth, we ourselves may at last know the consolation which they offer to those whom we have left.

I am the resurrection and the life: he that believeth on Me, though he die, yet shall he live; and whosoever liveth and believeth on Me shall never die. Believest thou this? The question is addressed to us no less than to Martha; and if, as we weigh the words, they seem to transcend our powers; if we dimly feel that they involve truths of which we can hold firmly but a very little; if they express, so far as we can interpret them, what we aspire towards as a splendid hope, rather than what we

Believest thou this? 101

have already made our own; let us not be disheartened. The answer of Martha may furnish us with the model for our own. *Yea Lord,* she said, *I have believed that thou art the Christ, the Son of God, even He that cometh into the world.* She had gained a measure of faith and she kept it still in her sorest distress. What had been won and used in happier times was her stay now. But she did not hasten to go beyond her experience. Her definite confession was bounded by her immediate knowledge. She had not as yet been enabled to regard the Lord in the aspect under which He now revealed Himself, as the Giver of life; and she did not prematurely express what she waited to learn. At the same time she implied that far more was included in what she already knew than she had yet realised. The issue confirmed her faith; and so will it be with us. Let us not attempt impatiently to affect a fulness of knowledge which we have not. Let us not rest in self-complacency at the point of spiritual perception which we have reached. Let us declare boldly and sincerely what we have been enabled to learn of Christ and then wait for wider intelligence. If we believe in a living Christ, the Son of God, that faith contains treasures of wisdom which later experience will teach us to make our own. The years as they pass may leave us a sad inheritance of weakness and death; but in due time Christ will reveal Himself to us,

VII. even here, in this chequered scene of loss and conflict, as the Resurrection and the Life, the Life whereby He quickens us for new labour, the Resurrection whereby He gives back to us the past transfigured for nobler uses.

VIII.

THE WAY, THE TRUTH, AND THE LIFE.

I am the way, and the truth, and the life: no one cometh unto the Father, but by Me.

ST JOHN xiv. 6.

THE two revelations of the Lord which we have still to consider differ in their circumstances from those which have gone before. They were given by Christ when the course of His public ministry was ended. He had withdrawn Himself from the world; and on the other side Judas had now left the group of Apostles, of which he was the one faithless member. The Last Supper was ended: the Son of Man was glorified: the separation of the Light and the darkness was complete. Without it was night: within was the brightness of joy felt to be on the point of fulfilment. The joy of the Master was clear and sure: the joy of the disciples was yet to be tested and purified. For through what agony the fulfilment was to come the Lord alone knew; and the words which He addressed to those whom He had chosen to be the founders of His Church were designed to prepare them for their sharpest and most unlooked for trial. He indeed had

VIII.

John xii. 36.
John xiii. 30.

won the victory, but they had to make good their part in it. And so He developed one all-sufficing thought through the discourses which occupied the last meeting-time in the upper chamber, and the last walk to Gethsemane, varying it in many ways, that it might answer to each phase of temptation:

John xvi. 33. *In the world ye shall have tribulation: but be of good cheer; I have overcome the world.* He and His disciples were now finally set on one side, and all the organised powers of selfishness on the other. Henceforward the conflict between them was to be waged on fresh conditions and with fresh powers. It is as if the words with which He called the eleven to join Him on His road to

John xiv. 31. Death—*Arise, let us go hence*—were at the same time a call to a new career, a new work, a new life, dawning upon them at last through the gloom in which their own aims and fancies were lost for ever.

If we bear this in mind we shall feel, more truly than we can do otherwise, how the revelation of the text corresponds with the crisis at which it was delivered. No sooner had the traitor gone out, than the Lord gave utterance to the strain of thanksgiving which told that the end was at hand. Then turning to His disciples with

John xiii. 31. a title of endearment—*my little children*—which stands alone in the Gospels, He warned them of coming separation, and desertion and death. By His address He shewed them that His own love—

the foundation of the new commandment of love —would survive His removal and would survive the failure of their boldest professions. But we can fancy with what an intensity of sadness they must have heard of open and immediate denial. What unknown weakness could there be in their own hearts? what unknown perils could there be in their path? For the moment hope must have been eclipsed by sorrow, till the familiar voice of consolation followed close upon the voice of warning. *Let not your heart be troubled. Believe in God: believe also in Me.* Cast aside, that is, every thought of self, which can only bring estrangement, defeat, humiliation: admit no misgivings of personal frailty: trust to no presumptuous promptings of personal confidence: look without you and not within: look to the Father whom I came to declare: look to Me, whom you have learnt to know. So will you perceive that I go to make ready for you a place in a heavenly home: that I go for a while in order that I may bring you to Me for ever: *and whither I go ye know the way.*

Dared the apostles to take to themselves this assurance? All might be plain; but they had erred too often before to be confident. At least it was not a time to affect knowledge. The questions at issue were too momentous to be left in vague uncertainty. Courage is not blindness and it is better a thousand fold to confess our doubts, our

John xiv. 1.

misgivings, our ignorance, that we may receive strength, and light, than to exclude the access of both by a proud assumption of intelligence. So Thomas found it both now and afterwards. *Lord,* he said, *we know not whither Thou goest; how know we the way?* He had come on the last journey to Jerusalem ready to die with his Lord, but, if it might be, he would die in the light. The frank confession of ignorance to an all-knowing, all-loving Lord was in itself an unspoken petition for such enlightenment as was possible. And the implied prayer was granted. *Jesus saith unto him I am the way, the truth, and the life: no man cometh unto the Father but by Me.*

Here was the answer to the thoughts by which the hearts of the disciples were troubled. They had reached the point at which (as they now knew) they were to lose the sensible presence of Him whom they had followed hitherto. The goal towards which they had been moving was still hidden. Under such circumstances advance might well seem to them to be impossible or fruitless. Must they not fear that when left alone they would find the world once more a trackless wilderness? Christ silenced these doubts when He said *I am the Way.* If the way were clear, they could pursue it boldly.

They had seen their earthly dreams fade away one by one. Messiah had claimed the homage of His people, and His people had rejected *the Truth, the Life.* 109

Him. Was it then to be believed that the old teaching, the age-long discipline of Israel, was unsubstantial and transitory? was nothing left of all the treasures of old time? Christ met these misgivings when He said *I am the Truth*. If the Truth remained, they could behold its fashion change without dismay.

They were soon to look upon Him who had called Lazarus from the grave dying upon the Cross. When that hour came, must they bow before death as the great conqueror? Were they to regard that which they saw as the end of all? Were they to hear without reply the mocking taunts of the rulers: *He saved others: let Him save Himself if He be the Christ of God.* Even on this darkest scene Christ threw the light of heaven when He said *I am the Life*. If the Life lived on, they could wait till it shewed itself in some new shape. So the conception of life was raised to its highest and final form. The Lord had already revealed Himself as sovereign over the fulness of personal being when He said *I am the Resurrection and the Life*, and now He revealed His wider kingdom in the prospect of His own death. In dying He lives.

And all that Christ said to the apostles on the eve of His Passion He has said and still says to men in every great crisis of history. The trial to which the first disciples were exposed was peculiar rather in its form than in its essential character.

VIII.

Luke xxiii. 35.

VIII. It was the trial which belongs to every period of transition. It was the trial which presses and will press most heavily upon our generation. And if we in our turn would face it, and come out victors from the contest, it can only be by listening with absolute devotion to the revelation of Christ which makes clear to us that there is a purpose running through all the ages and broadening upwards to the threshold of a Father's home: that there is an abiding reality underneath the shifting phenomena of the world which cannot be lost: that there is a law of coherence, of progress, of growth uniting in a harmonious whole movements, efforts, energies which appear to us to be broken, discordant, conflicting: it can only be by claiming for our own direct instruction, as charged with a new meaning and reaching to new realms, the words with which Christ answered the appeal of St Thomas: *I am the way, the truth and the life: no man cometh to the Father but by Me.*

We have indeed great need of the encouragement which the words bring. And we must not close our eyes to the need if we would realise the encouragement. Everywhere around us men are perplexed, uncertain, sense-bound; and if as yet the full violence of the storm has not burst upon us, we cannot be indifferent to perils which belong to our common nature though they are made more urgent by our position.

Men, I say, are perplexed. The infinite complexity, and hurry and intensity of modern life confuses our perception of its general tendency. The old paths appear to be lost in a wild maze. Eager voices call us to follow this track or that. If we pause for a moment, we are at once left behind by our fellow-travellers. There is no repose, no strength of quietness, no patient waiting for fuller knowledge. We are almost driven to ask if there be any way, any end at all before us? And if there be, whether it is not hopeless for us to look for it? At such times let us hearken to Christ's voice *I am the Way*, and then purpose and order will come back to the world. We shall see that through all the ages there does run one way of self-sacrifice, and that way is Christ. All other ways soon disappear. They are drawn to this or lost in the darkness. We may not be able to see more than a few steps before us, but if these lie not on self but on Christ, we can have no doubt of the issue. We may not be able to reconcile the movements of others with our own, but if we know that at each moment they rest on Christ, we know that their way is the same as ours. We may not be able to tell whither we are going, but it is enough that Christ has bridged over the chasm between earth and heaven, and that as we advance along the way which He made, and which He is, we shall sooner or later be admitted to the vision of God and reflect the brightness of His glory.

Men are uncertain. So much that has been held sacred for ages has been questioned or found false: so many social theories have been rudely scattered: so many noble traditions have been resolved into legends: so many popular interpretations of Holy Scripture have been found baseless; that, when we look round on the ruin of old beliefs, we can hardly wonder that the question should arise whether there is anything on which faith can still repose. When the trial is sorest the words of Christ, *I am the Truth,* at once lift us into that loftier region wherein no doubt or falsehood enters. Christ the Son of God and the Son of Man: Christ the Uniter of the seen and the unseen: Christ the Reconciler of the sinful and the Sinless: He is the Truth. In Him *is,* is essentially and eternally, all that is presented to us in the images of order and beauty and purity and love which surround us. If we hold to Him in His double Nature, as having lived and died and risen again for us, as having brought together into one all things in heaven and earth and beneath the earth, as revealing little by little through the clouds which rise from below larger prospects of His Person and His Work: we shall watch without fear for the issue of every controversy, sure of this that each result gained by honest and patient labour, each conclusion reached through self-

Christ the Life *to those bound by sense.*

denial and self-restraint, will teach us more of Him, and that time will cease before we have fully learnt our lesson.

Men are sense-bound. The claims of the world upon us are so many and so urgent: the triumphs of physical science are so unquestionable and so wide: the marvels of that which we can see and feel are so engrossing and inexhaustible; that it is not surprising that we should be tempted to rest in them: to take the visible for our heritage: to close up our souls against those subtle questionings whereby they strive after the knowledge of that which no eye hath seen or ear heard or hand felt, that life of the plant, of the man, of the world, which comes as we know not and goes as we know not. But strong as the charm may be to lull to sleep that which is noblest within us, the words of Christ, *I am the Life* can break it. We feel that that thought of a divine personality underlying outward things, quickening them, shaping them, preserving through dissolution the sum of their gathered wealth, answers to a want within us. It brings back to us the assurance that death cannot prevail for ever. It opens infinite visions of hope, which, if they stir us to loftier endeavour, strengthen us also to bear without despondency disappointment and failure for the moment. In their light we can work without shrinking from the labours by which we are burdened. In their light we can believe without striving impatiently to unravel the mysteries by which we are encompassed; we can work, and while we work we can believe and know that it is good for a man that he *should both hope and quietly wait for the salvation of the Lord.*

<small>Lam. iii. 26.</small>

I am the Way, the Truth and the Life: no man cometh unto the Father but by me. The last words which seem at first sight to narrow the magnificent prospect on which we are allowed to look, do in fact only define it. They do not set limits for the access to the Father but give us a wider view of the action of Christ. They carry light into the dark ages and dark places of the earth. They tell us that wherever there is heroic self-surrender, wherever there is devoted study of the ways and works even of an unknown God, wherever there is a heart yearning towards the undiscovered glories of a spiritual world, there is Christ: there is Christ though we see Him not, and His name is not named; and where Christ is, there is the approach to a loving Father.

The question indeed must often arise in our hearts whether the virtue of Christ's work is limited to those who consciously welcome the Gospel which proclaims it. Perhaps we can best gain the answer if we call to mind the declarations which are made of its widest efficacy. When St Paul speaks of the good pleasure of God *to sum up all things in Christ, the things in the heavens, and the things upon the earth;* and again, through

<small>Eph. i. 10.</small>

Him *to reconcile all things unto Himself, having made peace through the blood of His cross; through Him, whether things upon the earth or things in the heavens;* and when he describes this as the issue of the Lord's perfect obedience, *that in the name of Jesus every knee should bow, of things in heaven, and things on earth and things under the earth;* a prospect is opened which we have no authority, as we certainly can have no wish, to limit. We seem to see the blessing of a redeemed humanity communicated through the Church to other orders of being; and if this be so, we cannot doubt that in some way mankind shares in the blessing which is extended to creation. We have no powers to define such views in detail, but we may thankfully recognise that they are given to us, and place every fear and misgiving under the light which they afford.

<small>VIII. Col. i. 20. Phil. ii. 10. Eph. iii. 10; Rom. viii. 20 f.</small>

From these last and largest fulfilments of Christ's words and Christ's work, which we cannot as yet define clearly, we turn to those things which are written plainly for us. We have been placed upon the Way. We have been taught the Truth. We have been made partakers of the Life. The Way must be traversed: the Truth must be pursued: the Life must be realised. Then cometh the end. Our pilgrimage, long as it may be or short, if we have walked in Christ will leave us by the throne of God; our partial knowledge if we have looked upon all things in Christ will be lost in open sight; our little lives perfected, purified, harmonised in Him Whom we have trusted will become in due order parts of the one Divine Life, when God is all in all.

IX.

THE TRUE VINE.

I am the true vine.
I am the vine: ye are the branches.

ST JOHN xv. 1, 5.

WE saw in the last lecture that the two final revelations which the Lord gave of Himself differ from those which precede by the fact that they were not delivered 'in the world' but were addressed to the circle of faithful disciples after the departure of Judas, and designed to prepare them for immediate trial and future work. The revelation of Christ as *the Way, the Truth, and the Life* which we then considered was given in the upper-chamber after the Supper was ended: this of the Vine and the branches which comes before us now was given on the way to Gethsemane. And the revelation of Christ as *the true Vine* fitly closes the whole series. It brings into one vivid image the various lines of thought which we have hitherto pursued separately. It consecrates to new uses the symbolism of the Old Covenant. It offers a type of manifold, of combined, of fruitful energy. It presents to us Christ and the believers in Christ in their highest unity, as a living whole.

IX. He is no longer portrayed as apart from them, but as one with them, so that they are, to borrow the figure of St Paul, limbs of that divine Body of which He is the Head, the creative Law and the animating Life.

The Vine was one of the earliest and also one of the latest symbols of the Holy Land, and of the ancient Church.

Num. xiii. 23 f. The cluster of grapes from Eshcol was the sign of the fertility of Canaan to the expectant wanderers. The cluster of grapes and the vine-leaf were common emblems on the Maccabæan coins. A golden vine upon the gates was one of the most splendid ornaments of Herod's Temple. Israel was Ps. lxxx. 8. Jer. ii. 21. *a vine brought out of Egypt: a noble vine* which *grew degenerate*, according to the language of the Hos. xiv. 7. prophets, yet not without the hope of restoration. Among the writings of Isaiah no words are more Is. v. 1 ff. familiar than *the song of the beloved touching His vineyard*. Among the parables of the Lord no one moved the people more deeply than that of Matt. xxi. 33 ff and parr. the wicked husbandmen, who would have made the Lord's vineyard their own by the murder of the true heir. The thoughts of fifteen hundred years, thoughts of beauty, of growth, of luxuriance, of fertility, of joy, were gathered round the vine, and at the end Christ says in the passage before us that all those thoughts were fulfilled in Him: *I am the true*—the ideal—*vine.* 'In Me,' that is, 'in Me who have taken humanity to

An image of manifold life.

'Myself, all which men have seen in the life of
'the plant and transferred to themselves is realised·
'There is beyond all thought an innermost har-
'mony between the works of my Father. Those
'which you call lower, simpler, help you to rise to
'a fuller knowledge of the loftiest and most com-
'plex. The people of God have in very deed, like
'the Vine, a common being. They are distinguish-
'ed one from another like leaf and tendril by a
'rich variety. They are bound together by a vital
'unity. They are prepared for large fruitful-
'ness. Whatever the image of the vine has
'suggested to the teachers of old, whatever you
'have sought to express through it yourselves, is
'true. *I am the true Vine, and my Father is the
'husbandman....I am the Vine: ye are the branches.*'

Out of the many thoughts offered to us by this parallel of the life of the Christian Body with the life of the tree, there are three, as I have already indicated, which I wish specially to mark. It shews us that the Christian life—the life in Christ—is manifold: that it is one: that it is productive.

The Christian life—the Christian life that is in its widest sense—is manifold. The loveliness and grandeur and power of the Christian life all spring from the infinite variety of its forms. In some respects the Pauline image of the body and its members presents this lesson to us with more completeness; but the image of the vine—the tree— brings out one side of it which is lost there. In

IX.

1 Cor. vi. 15.
Rom. xii.
4 f.
Eph.. iv. 16; v. 30.

the tree we can actually trace how the variety is all fashioned out of one original element. Step by step we can see how the leaf passes into the flower, the fruit, the seed. However different the parts may be in the end, it can be shewn that they are essentially one, modified according to the work which they have to do. In the last change there are still marks of the beginning: in the first leaf there is, if we can read it aright, a prophecy of the tree. And more than this: not only are the separate parts thus related in their most extreme variation, but there is always a correspondence between the groupings of the parts which answers to the constitution of the whole plant. Not only is the petal for example truly a leaf, but the arrangement of the leaves round the stem indicates the arrangement of the petals in the flower. One law is fulfilled everywhere. There is no repetition in the organs which are most like: there is no discord in the organs which are most widely separated. It would be easy to follow out this divine plan, so to speak, of the tree's growth in much fuller detail; but what I have said is enough to shew the truths which it teaches us as to the diversities of our Christian life. Each living part of *the true vine* is ideally the same, and yet individually different. Our differences are given to us to fit us for the discharge of special offices in its life. If therefore we seek to obliterate them or to exaggerate them, we mar

its symmetry and check its fruitfulness. We may
perhaps have noticed how in a rose the coloured
flower-leaf sometimes goes back to the green stem-
leaf and the beauty of the flower is at once destroyed. Just so it is with ourselves. If we
affect a work other than that for which we are
made we destroy that which we ought to further.
Our special service, and all true service is the
same, lies in doing that which we find waiting to
be done by us.   There is need, as we know,
of the utmost energy of all. There is need of the
particular differences of all. We cannot compare
the relative value of the leaves, and the tendrils
and the flowers in the vine: it is healthy, and
vigorous, and fruitful because all are there. We
cannot clearly define the minute features by which
leaf is distinguished from leaf, or flower from flower,
but we can feel how the whole gains in beauty by
the endless combination of their harmonious contrasts.   From the figure we turn to ourselves;
and when we look upon our own restless and
ambitious strivings; upon our efforts to seem to
be what we are not; upon our unceasing mimic-
ries of those about us; upon our impatience of
the conditions of our little duties; can we venture
to think that we have learnt, as we yet may learn,
the first lesson of the Vine?

The second lesson flows directly from the first.
The Vine with its rich variety of parts, with its
sharp distinctions of function, is one Vine; one by

the actual combination of all its existing organs, one by the accumulated results of all its past life. Our own bodies are so transitory: we seem to stand so far apart one from the other: the sense of individuality within us is so much stronger and so much more obtrusive than the sense of dependence; that we are apt to lose sight of our intimate and indissoluble connexion with others as men and as Christian men. Here again the image of the tree comes to our assistance. Nothing could shew us more clearly that there is a unity between us as we now work together in our several places, and a unity between us and all who have gone before us. We are bound together in the present, even as the tree has one life, though the life is divided through a thousand forms, and we are children of the former time, even as the tree preserves in itself the results of its past life, which has reached, it may be, over a thousand years. These two ideas of a present unity and of a historic unity are not equally easy to grasp. We can all see the present unity of the parts of the tree: we can all rise from that to the conception of the unity of men in the nation or in the Church. However imperfectly the idea is worked out in thought, however imperfectly it is realised in practice, yet it is not wholly strange or ineffective among us. But that other unity, the unity of one generation with another which has been and with another which hereafter will be, is as yet un-

includes the past and the present. 125

familiar to most men. The tree may help us to learn it. Cut down the tree, and you will read its history in the rings of its growth. We count and measure them and reckon that so long ago was a year of dearth, so long ago a year of abundance. The wound has been healed but the scar remains to witness to its infliction. The very moss upon its bark tells how the trunk stood to the rain and the sunshine. The direction of its branches reveals the storms which habitually beat upon them. We call the whole perennial and yet each year sees what is indeed a new tree rise over the gathered growths of earlier time and die when it has fulfilled its work.   And all this is true of the society of men. We are what a long descent has made us. Times of superstition and misgovernment and selfish indulgence have left and ever will leave their marks upon us. There are unhealthy parts on which the cleansing light has not fallen. There are distorted outgrowths which have suffered from want of shelter and want of care. And there are too, let us thank God for it, solid and substantial supports for developments yet to come: great boughs, as it were, towering heavenward, through which our little results of life may be borne aloft: ripe fruits which may be made the beginnings of wider vitality through our service. Here indeed does the word find its perfect fulfilment, *One soweth and another reapeth.*   This great thought, and I do not think

IX.

John iv. 37.

that any thought is more worthy to be taken to heart by us just now, is most humbling and yet most stirring. If we reflect on the magnificent inheritance which we have received—on our English language, for example, which even as we speak it quickens our souls though we know it not with the life of countless generations—shall we not at once render devout praise to God for the great things which He has done for us through our fathers, and beseech Him with an intensity of supplication that He will enable us to transmit to our children the wealth which we have received, purified, if it may be, from some dross by our sufferings, and increased by our labours.

For there is yet a third lesson of the Vine. The diversity of its parts, the unity of its life, are turned to one end: that it may be fruitful. *He that abideth in me,* Christ said, *and I in him bringeth forth much fruit.* The tree which is the image of the Christian society is not a wild tree. The watchful care of the Great Husbandman trains and prunes and tends it. If the vital power is misused, it is withdrawn. The branch which interferes with the due growth of others is cut off. There is no need to interpret these speaking figures. They appeal at once to our consciences. A Christian who is not fruitful is no Christian. The widest and grandest views of our faith, such as this revelation of the Lord through the Vine opens to us, are not given only

Christ lives in the Christian.

to fill our imaginations, but to move us to action. And there is a marvellous beauty in the aspect under which they present the last results of the Christian life. These are from this point of view in the strictest sense fruits and not works. They are seen to belong, that is, to the operation of an indwelling immanent power, and not to the exercise of personal will. They are, so to speak, the spontaneous, necessary, natural, outcome of what the Christian truly is. When he is regarded in himself, then the notion of design, of effort, of work rightly comes in; but when, as here, he is regarded in his essential relation to Christ then all he does, all he can do, is the due effect of that life with which he is inspired.

And this thought brings me to the last point which I wish to notice. We have spoken of the three lessons of the Vine, but we have not yet placed them in direct connexion with the inmost being of the Vine itself. Christ said I *am the true Vine*. The diversity of the Christian society is thus a revelation of Christ's fulness: its unity is a revelation of Christ's life: its fruitfulness is a revelation of Christ's power.

Our loftiest speculations fall far short of the mystery involved in this oneness of the Vine and the branches, according to which, as St Paul says, Col. i. 24. the believer fills up what is lacking in that which Christ hath suffered and made possible for him. But when we can as yet see little we can trust entirely; and it is in this thought, that Christians do in some sense carry out, embody, complete the work of Christ through His presence, that we find our confidence: our strength: our hope. Our confidence because we are sure that if we offer ourselves, as we are, to God in Christ, God will find an office for us to discharge. Our strength, because we know that that lives on with an unending growth which He has received and hallowed. Our hope, because we believe that in due time, sooner or later, others will gather the produce which we have prepared and bless Him for labours to which we shall see no harvest.

For we must not forget that as yet there remains a season of trial and pain. We are at present called to struggle against all that within us which rebels against the first principles of religious life, dependence and fellowship. The self-willed must suffer separation from Christ: the faithful must look for discipline that they may become more abundantly fruitful. But it is sufficient for us that our *Father is the husbandman* and that we are branches of Christ.

Temptation will come: failure will come: disappointment will come. There will be the sharp sorrow, when something is taken away on which we have prided ourselves. There will be the bitter reproach, when we look back on what we have lost through our own neglect. There will be the blank regret, when the end for which we have worked patiently is hidden from our eyes. But deeper than all sorrow, stronger than all reproach, more sovereign than all regret, the words will remain with us,

I am the Vine, and my Father is the husbandman.

I am the Vine, ye are the branches.

Herein, that is, in your abiding in Me, *is my Father glorified, that ye may bear much fruit.*

X.

THE VISION OF CHRIST THE VISION OF THE FATHER.

He that hath seen Me hath seen the Father.

St John xiv. 9.

IN the foregoing lectures we have been allowed to consider in some detail the various personal revelations of the Lord which are recorded in the Gospel of St John. I desire now to gather them up, if it may be, into one summary view, and connect them all with the central Truth which they are designed to illuminate, the revelation of the Father. At the beginning we saw that Christ spoke of His mission as being undertaken in His Father's name: now at the close He declares in language of which we can barely touch the meaning, *He that hath seen Me hath seen the Father*. His Life, His works, His words were not only directed to teach men something about the Father, but to shew the Father to men: not only to describe the object of our love and worship and faith, but actually to present Him, so that we may never lose His living Presence.

x.

John v. 43.

And this revelation came at a crisis of necessity. Up to the Incarnation the religious history of men is little more than the history of the gradual withdrawal of God from the world. Apart from the Incarnation that sad history must go forward till it ends in a complete separation of earth and heaven. And if we reflect what we are, we can feel how the discipline of that withdrawal answered to the development of our nature: we can feel how the Advent of the Son of God answered to the full disclosure of our wants. Step by step as the conceptions of the Creator and Preserver grow loftier and larger He Himself seems to be taken farther from us till He comes to us as a Saviour.   In this respect the experience of the individual is the experience of the race. Our childly thoughts of God picture Him in very close connexion with ourselves. We extend to the unseen order the image of the relations with which we are most familiar. We make in our own simple ways covenants with God, even as the patriarchs made them, and He no less surely blesses them.   But as years go on wider views of society, new duties, new temptations open upon us. In accordance with this inevitable change in our position we regard God differently. He appears to us under more general attributes, as Lawgiver and King. We reach the stage which the people of Israel reached when through their ritual and their national life they were trained to find in the God of their Fathers, the God of all the nations of the earth. The days

a withdrawal of God.

of sensible communing with God may have gone. The open vision may be no more seen. The light may have ceased to flash intelligibly from the highpriest's breastplate. But there are still living prophetic voices. The word of the Lord comes with an authoritative voice to cheer or to condemn. We do not however rest even here. As it was with the nation, so it is with the man. A time of divine silence follows. We are left to ponder over that which has hitherto been made known to us. Then comes the sorest trial. We strive, in proportion as we have learnt our earlier lessons well, to look more closely at ourselves, at the world, at God. And as we look great mysteries take shape before us. The mystery of sin: how can its stain be done away? the mystery of law: how can we reconcile our freedom with the inexorable rule of sequence which we observe? the mystery of the Infinite: how can we conceive of the ineffable majesty of the Almighty in fellowship with weak transitory creatures of earth such as we are? Most of us, I fancy, have known something of these questionings. We have found in our own hearts the spirit of the old Jewish sects. Happy, thrice happy, if when we have been most burdened, most perplexed, most humbled, we have heard the Gospel which has been made articulate by our sorrows; and listened to the words of Christ which bring back all tender love, all trustful confidence, all aspiring hope, *He*

x.

1 Sam. iii. 1.

that hath seen Me hath seen the Father. In Him there is atonement. In Him there is freedom. In Him there is unity. We seek for that which shall do away with corruption, which shall inspire life, which shall bring us to God; and He says *I have overcome the world. Because I live ye shall live also. I and the Father are one.* Look to Me, so he speaks to us, as you have known Me; and in Me and through Me you will discern in clear and ineffaceable lineaments the likeness of the Father, not My Father only, but your Father for Whom you seek, so far as man can discern Him. The years will come and go. You will learn your own nature more thoroughly. You will feel more devoutly the grandeur of creation. You will grow in knowledge of the holiness of God. But all self-distrust, all progress, all penitence will bring out more and more brightly the infinite meaning of this the last revelation, till the veil be removed for ever. *He that hath seen Me hath seen the Father.*

If then the various titles of the Lord which have been brought before us, have helped us in any way to see Him more clearly, just so far they have helped us to see the Father also more clearly. Each one in succession has contributed in some measure to define that idea of a divine Fatherhood which is now given back for ever to mankind. This is what I wish now to mark; and in this connexion the titles so far as we need regard *a revelation of the Father's patience.*

them fall into three groups. The first title—the
Christ—shews us the Father preparing, so to
speak, the revelation of Himself. The next five
—the Bread of Life, the Light of the world, the
Door, the Good Shepherd, the Resurrection and
the Life—shew us the Father dealing with individuals. The last two—the Way the Truth and
the Life, the Vine—shew us the Father in relation
to the society of men. There is the lesson of the
Father's patience: the lesson of the Father's love:
the lesson of the Father's discipline.   Patience,
love, discipline are no doubt everywhere blended
together with infinite wisdom, and still as we
look at the Lord we see the separate attributes
of Fatherhood offered to us one by one for our
comfort and strengthening and guidance.

He that hath seen Christ hath seen the
Father's patience.   The very name *Christ*,
as we saw, bears witness to a promise slowly
shaped through two thousand years. In that
title we can thankfully acknowledge the sign that
in spiritual matters God deals with us as we can
bear His action. Not all at once, not in blinding
glory, not in overpowering might, but in many
parts and in many fashions, He trains His
children to a riper understanding of His counsels.   And in this education of the world
God works with watchful constancy even where
His Fatherhood is not openly recognised. When
Christ said *My Father worketh hitherto and I*

x.

John v. 17.

138 *The revelation of Christ*

X. *work*, he set before us the teaching of that other title—the Word—in which St John expresses his own view of the eternal Being of Christ, and shews God speaking through Him to the hearts of all men, speaking to them through the life of creation, moving them to claim the prerogative of sons. Thus whether it be among *those who are called by His name*, or among those who *ignorantly worship* Him, there is one law of never hasting, never resting progress in the working of God through His Son. He who has in any way seen the Lord as the Christ, and as the Word, has seen the Father's patience.

Is. xliii. 7.

Acts xvii. 23.

He that hath seen Christ hath also seen the Father's love. This indeed we all confess, and confess at the same time how little we can really understand of the amazing truth that *God hath sent His only begotten Son into the world that we might live through Him*. But while this truth in its fulness wholly transcends our power of distinct thought, the various revelations of Christ which we have examined shew us how the love of God in Him follows us in all the vicissitudes and needs of our earthly life, sustaining, teaching, sheltering, guiding us, and at last clothing us with immortality.

1 John iv. 9.

Day by day and hour by hour we are made aware of our frailty, of our decay, of the transitoriness of all things visible. Through suffering and sorrow and loss the words of Christ come to us:

a revelation of the Father's love. 139

As the living Father sent Me and I—I, the Incarnate Son—*live because of the Father, so he that eateth Me, even he shall live because of Me.* We may that is even now share in a life of which the Father is the one object and the one source, a life which comes to us because the Son is Son, because the Father is Father. The love of the Father in the Son gives life.

X.
John vi. 57.

We are perplexed by a strange conflict of ways and opinions. Shadows, mists, clouds gather about us. We cannot but pause in bewilderment as to our course, till the words of Christ come to us across the gloom: *He that followeth Me shall not walk in darkness but shall have the light of life...I am not alone, but I and the Father that sent Me.* The love of the Father in the Son gives light.

John viii. 12, 16. Comp. xvi. 32.

We are occupied and distracted by the cares and duties of the world. We dare not shake them off and yet we doubt whether they can be reconciled with higher claims upon us. The words of Christ shew where lies the security of the faithful heart: *I am the door; by Me, if any man enter in he shall be saved and shall go in and out and find pasture...That which my Father hath given unto Me is greater than all.* To be gathered in His fold is a consecration of all work. The love of the Father in the Son gives shelter.

John x. 29.

We know our wanderings. Again and again we go astray. We are tempted to think that our wilfulness and waywardness have withdrawn us

140   *The revelation of Christ*

x.
John x.
14 f.

from our Master's regard. Christ's words again bring assurance to the despondent: *I am the good Shepherd and know my sheep and am known of mine, even as the Father knoweth Me and I know the Father.* No perversity can exhaust that tenderness: no weakness can escape that knowledge. The relation of the believer to the Son answers to the relation of the Son to the Father. The love of the Father in the Son gives confidence.

Then at last there remains the stern necessity of death. But the love of the Father which has been with us hitherto remains even there. The words which Christ uttered by the grave of Lazarus, when He saw life where others imagined corruption, were spoken for all time: *Father, I thank Thee that Thou hast heard Me.* In them the revelation of love is consummated in the face of man's supreme trial. The love of the Father in the Son gives resurrection.

John xi. 41.

He then that hath seen Christ hath seen the Father's patience and the Father's love: he hath seen also the Father's discipline.

There is, as we observed, a startling sound in the sentence, *No man cometh to the Father but by Me;* and yet we feel that it must be so. Doubtless the action of Christ is far wider and far more varied than we can at present perceive; but without Him man must be lost in self. It is only by coming out of ourselves, by recognising the fact of larger connexions, by treading with firm

John xiv. 6.

a revelation of the Father's discipline. 141

foot upon the way of sacrifice, by entering, that is,   x.
into fellowship with the Son of man, as the
Father draws us, that we can come to Him, Whom
we are taught to address as *Our Father*, claiming
for others the Sonship which we claim for ourselves.

We cannot therefore choose our own way of
approaching God; and as we draw near to Him,
we must leave ourselves in His hands. The access
is by self-surrender; and the service of others is
the law of our later action. *I am the vine and* John xv.
my Father is the husbandman. I am the Vine, ye 1, 5.
are the branches. This, as we saw in the last
lecture, is the figure of our Christian service.
There is no isolation in the manifold variety of
our offices. There is no uniformity in the absolute
oneness of our life. Separation for the unfruitful:
cleansing, pruning, for the fruitful, such is the
law of the Father's discipline. And of Christ
Himself it is written that *though He were a Son* Hebr. v. 8.
*yet learned He obedience by the things which He
suffered;* even as He said, *I came down from* John vi.
heaven not to do mine own will, but the will of Him 38.
that sent me.

The will of the Father, that is, is made known
to us as we can understand it in the will of Christ;
and so we are brought back to His words: *He
that hath seen Me hath seen the Father.* Each
of the various revelations which we have now
rapidly brought together helps us, I think, in

due measure to realise this central Truth of our Theology. One by one they enable us to be sure that in looking to Christ we look to the Father, that in living in Christ we live in the Father. They bring back to us all that our affections cling to as alone sufficient to support our human faith.

In the earliest ages God was pleased to satisfy man's instincts by transferring to Himself in a figure the senses and feelings of men. The saints of old time, with childlike minds, rejoiced to think that His 'eye' was upon them: that His 'ear' was open to their prayers. The thought of His 'wrath' or 'jealousy' moved them with wholesome fear: the thought of His 'compassion' and 'repentance' raised them from hopeless despair. It was as easy as it was vain for philosophy to point out that in all this they were extending finite ideas to an infinite Being. They could not surrender what was the soul of religion. And when the fulness of time came, all that had been figure before was made reality. Christ in His own Person reconciled the finite and the infinite: man and God. By virtue of His Incarnation we know that all which belongs to the perfection of humanity has a true union with Deity. God in Christ gives back to us all that seemed to have been lost by the necessary widening of thought through the progress of the ages. We can without misgiving apply the language of

given back and hallowed in Christ. 143

human feeling to Him Whom we worship. We can give distinctness to the object of our adoration without peril of idolatry. The limitations of our being do not measure the truth but they are made fit to express it for us. Christ seated at the right hand of the Father is no less man in His unspeakable glory than He was *in the days of His flesh.* We aspire and hope, and He receives our earthly homage and lifts it above earth. We struggle and fall, and He with the sympathy of a common nature strengthens and raises us. We are bereaved and then pass away ourselves, and He unites and quickens all who trust in Him with the power of His undying life. In Him all that touches us with tenderest devotion is reconciled with all that awes us with the most devout reverence. We turn again and again to the portraiture of His divine presence which lives in the Gospels, to every trait of holiness, of sacrifice, of mercy, of calm reproof and gracious encouragement, and we know that in these we have the image of our Father.

And the portraiture to which we turn is not for passive contemplation, but for the inspiration and the transfigurement of our whole being. As we look at the living Lord with a truer conviction that we may even now reflect something of its likeness: with a simpler faith that we can find in Christ, the Son of God, the Son of man, the stay, the test, the object of our worship: with a

marginal notes: x. — Hebr. v. 7.

livelier assurance that in Him we too are partakers of the Divine Nature; we shall know—know with a knowledge which grows with all the growth of years—that it was for us, for our peace, for our joy, for our life Christ spake the words: *He that hath seen Me hath seen the Father.*

APPENDIX I.

THE TESTIMONY OF JESUS THE SPIRIT OF PROPHECY.

The testimony of Jesus is the spirit of prophecy.

REV. xix. 10.

THE testimony of Jesus is the spirit of prophecy. APP. I.
These words of the Apocalypse lay open to us the present power and the unalterable meaning of the Bible. On the one hand, they bring the divine message into the very centre of our life. On the other, they reveal to us the unchanging purpose which underlies the manifold shapes in which the message found expression in old time. The context in which the words occur adds to their impressiveness. The great enemy of the Church has fallen. The song of victory has been raised. The marriage feast of the Lamb is ready; and the angel who has ministered to the seer this vision of exceeding glory, pronounces the blessedness of those who are called to share in the triumph at length realised; and affirms that this is, indeed, the very will of God. Overwhelmed by the thought of such a revelation, the Apostle fell at the feet of him who made it, that he might worship him. *See thou do it not*, was the reply of the angel: *I am*

thy fellow servant, and of thy brethren that have the testimony of Jesus: worship God: for the testimony of Jesus is the spirit of prophecy. It is as if he would say: There is no such gulf as you picture to yourself between me and thee: there is but one full utterance of God proclaimed in many tones from the foundation of the world. He who confesses the Son of Man, *Jesus Christ come in the flesh,* has grasped all that the powers of heaven can bestow: he has attained to that knowledge which is life: he has been admitted to the direct contemplation of the glory of the Lord, and stands among His noblest ministers. *The testimony of Jesus,*—the witness to that which He is, and to that which He has done, in its eternal significance—*is the spirit of prophecy.* There is nothing greater than this, nothing beyond this, in the thoughts of the celestial hosts. The men of old time, who were moved by the Holy Spirit, had nothing but this to declare in figure and parable and dark saying. This revelation, this recognition, of the Person of Christ unites all created beings in an equality of adoring love. And the believer in every age is entitled to claim fellowship with angels and prophets and apostles in virtue of the truth to which he bears witness.

The words have thus, as I said, a double meaning: the two clauses which they form are convertible. It is true that the testimony of Jesus is the spirit of prophecy: that this testi-

The spirit of prophecy the testimony of Jesus.

mony which is now plainly delivered by the Church is the sum of all that was spoken aforetime in many portions and in many ways. And again it is true that the spirit of prophecy is the testimony of Jesus: that this spirit, this celestial impulse, this inner life of every divine voice, was derived from one source and directed to one end.

At present I wish to dwell chiefly on the second thought. I wish to lead some who may be troubled by difficulties of detail in the Old Testament to strive after a more comprehensive view of its character, to consider what St John encourages us to call its spirit. There are difficulties in the Old Testament, difficulties which perhaps we cannot explain. We have no desire to extenuate or to hide them. It would be strange if we had; for it is through these, as we believe, that we shall in due time learn to know better God's way of dealing with us. But we are also bound to remember that the Old Testament offers to us something far higher, deeper, more majestic, more inspiring, than materials for literary problems. The Old Testament, on any theory as to the origin of the writings which it contains, shews to us before all other books the philosophy of history in representative facts and in conscious judgments. It opens to us the prospect of one purpose variously reflected in writings spread over a thousand years: of one purpose moving onwards with a continuous growth among

APP. I. the barren despotisms of the east: of one purpose fulfilled in an unbroken national life which closed only when its goal was reached. The records in which this history is contained are strangely contrasted in style, in composition, in scope. They are outwardly disconnected, broken, incomplete: they belong to different ages of society: they are coloured by the natural peculiarities of different temperaments: they appeal to different feelings. But still in spite of this fragmentariness which seems to exclude the possibility of vital coherence: in spite of this variety which seems to be inconsistent with the presence of one informing influence, they shew a continuity of progressive life which is found nowhere else, even in a dream. They enable us to see the chosen people raised step by step through failure and rebellion and disaster to a higher level, furnished with larger conceptions of truth, filled with nobler ideas of a spiritual kingdom, fitted at last to offer to the Lord the disciples who should be the first teachers of His Gospel, and to provide a home where, as we read, *Jesus advanced in wisdom... and favour with God and man.* The world can shew no parallel to this divine growth, no parallel to this divine narrative of a divine growth, in all the stirring annals of time. The great monarchies rose and fell around the little Jewish state. Other nations shone with more conspicuous glory, but the people of God lived on.

Luke ii. 52.

The spirit of the Old Testament.

They were not endowed with splendid gifts which at once command the admiration of this world. They appealed to no triumphs of victorious enterprise; they reared no monuments of creative art. They were divided, oppressed, carried captive, *persecuted but not forsaken, cast down but not destroyed.* By the power of their consecration they lived on; by the power of that *spirit of prophecy* which was in them they converted to the service of their faith the treasures of their conquerors; they lived on because they *saw the invisible*, and they were inspired to interpret for all who should come after the law of their life.

What then, we ask, are the characteristics of this spirit of prophecy, of this spirit of the Old Testament, of which we speak? What are the main ideas by which Israel witnessed for centuries to the future advent of Christ? Briefly, I think, these: that Spirit witnessed to the unity of the human race as made by God in His own image; and it witnessed further to the belief that God would of His own love, and in His own wisdom, bring man and men into conformity with Himself. 'God is the one Creator of men : God is the one King of men.' These thoughts breathe through the Old Testament from beginning to end. These thoughts Christ the Son of Man fulfilled. By these thoughts *the spirit of prophecy* and *the testimony of Jesus* are shewn to be related as promise and accomplishment.

It is most important to dwell upon this universality of what I will call the Gospel of Creation, the Gospel of the Hexaemeron. No view of Judaism can be more false than that which seems to be most common, that it was essentially exclusive. It was exclusive, and necessarily exclusive, so far as it was a beginning, a preparation, a discipline. But it was always pointing to a consummation. It was exclusive in its decay and fall, when general faithlessness had reduced it to the level of a sect. But *from the first it was not so.* The structure of the Law was based upon that revelation which presents to us, in the opening chapters of Genesis, the largest views of the loving sovereignty of God, and of the divine origin and destiny of mankind. All that came after was ruled by these constituent principles of the spiritual life, and ministered to their establishment. On these the eye of faith rested during the shifting scenes of later progress. Towards the fulfilment of these the great leaders of the chosen people strove through every vicissitude of history. So it was that the Jewish nation stood among the kingdoms of the world as the herald of a coming unity, the asserter of a divine order. Its work was not for itself alone, but for humanity. By this prophetic, may I not say by this Messianic, character it was distinguished from Egypt, the representative of selfish wisdom, and from Babylon, the representative of selfish power. For the idea of Judaism, the power of the life of Israel, and the law of its growth, is seen not in the covenant from Sinai but in the covenant with Abraham. In the call and separation of the first patriarch we have the beginning of the Church—the *ecclesia*—the congregation gathered for the exercise of divine privileges—the beginning of history, the true exodus, the heavenward journey, entered upon in obedience to the divine bidding. The lessons which the record of Christ's work displays—the brotherhood of men, the fall of man, the Providential destiny of man—all lie as in a parable in that unique event. Dimly and partially we can understand how Abraham exulted in the effort to see Christ's day. When the Lord said unto him: *Get thee out of thy country and from thy kindred.... And in thee shall all families of the earth be blessed*, the great truths which Christ consummated by His coming were presented in a historic elementary form. The two most familiar names by which the patriarch is known, "the friend of God," and "the father of the faithful," mark for ever the conditions of the divine life. The redemption of the world, the redemption of the believer, are seen to start from a creative act. The Lord chooses; He declares His will; He manifests His purpose. And man, on his part, accepts the word which comes to his soul with instant, unhesitating obedience and trust. The relation between God and man is thus shewn to be personal; it is shewn to require effort, faith, sacrifice; it is shewn to obtain an immediate fulfilment in present duties.

In these truths then which present in outline the relation of man to God, as made by Him, separated from Him, born for Him, lies *the spirit of prophecy*. And the writings of the Bible— the Law, the Prophets, and the Psalms—embody them in various forms. There may be uncertainties as to the origin and date of different books: there may be doubts as to the interpretation of particular phrases which they contain. But *the spirit of prophecy* is something which rises above the region of such perplexities. It is the life of a nation: it is in a true sense the life of the world, which the nation took up into itself at the crises of its course. The great ideal of absolute communion of man and God was first offered and then slowly wrought out. The Promise was followed by the Law: the revelation was brought within narrow limits in order that a sure groundwork might be laid for the future fabric. There was a movement backward, as we regard it, that men might advance to the end by the orderly processes of life.

For the naturalness, the solidity, if I may so speak, of the spiritual progress of Israel is not less remarkable than its breadth. It is possible to find in the great teachers of other nations premature and fragmentary visions of truth, sometimes more attractive in themselves than the corresponding parts of the Old Testament; but they are visions premature and fragmentary. The Old Testament teaches by facts, by the organic and continuous development of a body. The LORD is not an abstraction, but a King, speaking, chastening, saving. The theatre of man's highest energies is not an imaginary Elysium of souls, but the earth with all its trials and contradictions. The prospect of the invisible future is almost excluded, lest men should forget that the world and all the powers of the world have to be conquered. One eternal counsel is carried forward, interpreted, applied, as those can bear it to whom its practical fulfilment is entrusted. The element of order remains in the minute provisions of an exacting ritual. The element of progress is provided in the utterances of the prophets who lay open the future in the present. All along the witness to a historic human Saviour, as the necessity and the hope of mankind, is written as the message of God through His Old Covenant. Even in the agonies of conflict one voice finds clear expression in word and deed,—in Moses, in Joel, in Haggai—that Israel had a mission to the world, as a first-born among many brethren.

Such a discipline, such a record of the discipline as we have, is, I say again, without parallel. Perhaps I feel tempted to envy those who have

156 *The history of Judaism*

APP. I. yet a life to give to their investigation. But I cannot dwell on details now. I ask you only to reflect at leisure how these thoughts of the personal action of God, of the living government of God, of the significance of the present life, are set out in the books of the Old Testament; how they take shape and enter into the conscience of the Jewish nation; how they find their last and fullest expression at the Return; and how then a time of silent waiting, of loneliness, almost of desolation, follows, in which it seems as if the hope by which the nation had lived was now exhausted. The LORD was then withdrawn, as it were, into light unapproachable. The heathen
Eccles. i. powers had triumphed. *Vanity* was written over
2.   the aims and achievements of men.

But even this period of silence, this latest stage in the preparatory economy, was an essential part of the witness of Judaism. It was necessary that it should be seen that the fellowship of God and man could not be consummated by visions and words; that the idea of holiness, the one sufficient end of being, could not be realised in the way of nature; that the destiny of man could not be accomplished in the narrow scene of earth. The prophecy appeared more distinct as it became isolated. Men recognised the ideal hope, but the fulfilment lingered.   Thus, even to the last, each successive stage of Jewish history disclosed with increasing clearness one supreme issue, which was felt to be more indispensable as it passed farther from attainment. The Gospel, a mystery above anticipation, was the only way of meeting aspirations and doubts which seemed alike to be invincible. By that at last the Presence to which we do reverence in the Law and the Prophets, was openly revealed and made perpetual. In the Person of Christ, God has been brought nearer to man than when He communed with the patriarchs. In the Person of Christ the divine righteousness, which was shadowed in ordinances, was made luminous. In the Person of Christ the present age and the age to come, the seen and the unseen, were united.

Let anyone think patiently over the unquestionable course of this history which I have tried to indicate; let him compare it with the history of any præ-Christian nation; let him study it in the personal confessions of the Psalter; let him observe how unexpectedly, how persistently, new elements contribute to its fulness without disturbing its direction; let him, in a word, strive to concentrate his attention upon the life, of which the Bible is the record, and not upon the record itself, and I venture to affirm that the thoughts will rise in his soul, to which Jacob gave utterance when he had seen in a vision earth and heaven united: *Surely the Lord is in the place and I knew it not.* Gen. xxviii. 16.

Most of us, I suppose, remember the answer

158 *Importance of dwelling first on the life*

APP. I.

Rom. xi. 22.

which was given to the Prussian king, who asked for the briefest and most convincing summary of the evidences of Christianity. It was simply this "Your Majesty, the Jews." He who so replied was thinking of Israel scattered and yet unabsorbed, rent into a thousand fragments and yet one, crushed and yet instinct with an intense life, an old church existing side by side with the new church as a witness to *the goodness and severity of God.* But the answer is still more powerful if we reflect on Israel moving through two thousand years toward the Advent of Messiah, feeling from age to age after the loftiest conception of a divine kingdom, receiving, through manifold disappointments and failures, fresh promises, clinging through defeat and disaster to the conviction that it was the depository of universal blessing. It is impossible, I repeat, for anyone to regard that history in its majestic and indisputable outlines without feeling that it was guided to some end. It is impossible to imagine any end able to reconcile all the aspirations which it raised, to solve all the enigmas which it brought into full light, than that which is given to us in the Birth, and Passion, and Resurrection of Christ. *The testimony of Jesus is the spirit of prophecy.*

If then it is certain that the writings of the Old Testament offer to us many grave difficulties which we are at present unable to overcome, it is no less certain that they offer a revelation of a purpose and a presence of God which bears in itself the stamp of truth. The difficulties lie in points of criticism; the revelation is given in the facts of a people's life. And in the trials of our present time, in the prospect of the work which we are called to do, it is our wisdom and our strength to turn to those old records of a divine discipline. The Gospel has made their meaning clearer than before, and brought home to us the truths which they embody. The lessons of national duty and of national responsibility, of selfishness and sacrifice, of sin and faith, are not obsolete. Nay, rather they are becoming day by day of more overwhelming importance. As Christians we have to do our part towards the hastening of the Lord's coming, as members of a great commonwealth and of a great Church, we have social obligations which we cannot disregard with impunity. The past has been interpreted; the greater glory of the future is shewn in the greater power which has been given to us for its realisation. The prophet's work has still to be done by those who have the prophet's spirit. And that spirit is not denied us. *The testimony of Jesus is the spirit of prophecy.*

It would have been hard—and we may thank God that we are spared the trial—to acknowledge a Galilean Teacher, as He moved among men in His infinite humility, to be the Son of God. It is hard still to find that He is with us, to discern

160 *The lesson of the life to be used still.*

APP. I. His message in lessons perhaps as strange as those which startled His first hearers; to recognise His form in those whom fashion despises.   Yet is it not the duty to which we are called? Is not this the office for which we have been furnished with a divine equipment? The last voice of the Lord has not been spoken. The last victory of the Lord has not been won.   We have known the facts of which all divine utterances are the exposition: we have looked upon the end in which all other ends are included. For us the dark and mysterious sayings of lawgiver, and seer, and psalmist, have been changed into the simple message of that which has been fulfilled among men: for us the language of struggling hope has been changed into the confession of historic belief: for us, not only as the confirmation of our faith, but as the guide of our Christian effort, *the testimony of Jesus is the* spirit *of propehcy*.

My brethren, to hear and to bear this testimony in the language of our time is that which we have to do. Every day brings us the occasion for our message. Every place offers to us the scene of our conflict. Testimony is indeed only another name for martyrdom. But He who armed with strength and crowned with glory His witnesses in old time will not fail us, if we in our hour of trial rest wholly upon Him.

St Mary's, Cambridge,
22nd SUNDAY AFTER TRINITY.

APPENDIX II.

THE REVELATION OF THE GLORY OF GOD; THE ANNUNCIATION AND THE RESURRECTION.

The glory of the LORD shall be revealed and all flesh shall see it together: for the mouth of the LORD hath spoken it.

ISAIAH xl. 5.

THE glory of the Lord shall be revealed and all flesh shall see it. These words, as it will be remembered, give the theme of the Gospel of the Old Testament, that 'Gospel before the Gospel' which is contained in the second part of Isaiah where prophecy finds its crown and consummation. No possible conclusions of criticism can affect the unique majesty of the vision of great hope which rises out of them. Questions of date and authorship sink wholly into the background in view of the truths which the prophet declares. Let any one read that Gospel of national life as a whole in its environment, and he will find what inspiration is: he will find what prophecy is: the sight of God and the living interpretation of the world in the light of His Presence. The situation is clear, whether it be foreseen or only seen: the promise is clear: the fulfilment is clear. Looking upon a poor band of exiles, isolated from all the services of their religion, deprived of their natural leaders, corrupted by apostasy which assumed the

APP. II. disguise of pious worship, crushed by an idolatrous tyranny, and shewing the vices of slaves, the prophet looks also upon the LORD, the God of their fathers, and by His Spirit he is enabled to read in suffering the lesson of hope, and to proclaim to a faithful remnant their mission to the nations.   Never, I believe, has patriotism been shewn in a nobler aspect than in these burning appeals to the future heirs of the divine promise. It is called out as the passion for human service and not for selfish dominion. The Deliverance which the prophet anticipates is wrought not by heroic effort but in the order of providence through an alien conqueror. The Victory of the liberated people which he describes comes not through force but through martyrdom. The end to which he points is not temporal sovereignty but the open acknowledgment of the God of Israel, a new heaven and a new earth.   There is, and he does not hide one dark trait, there is on all sides gloom and distrust and superstition and forgetfulness of God, but he proclaims with the assurance of one who has looked upon the Eternal, that *the Glory of the Lord shall be revealed, and all flesh shall see it together.*

The glory of the Lord : the phrase is a key-word of Scripture. The whole record of revelation is a record of the manifestation of God's glory. The Bible is one widening answer to the prayer of Moses, *Shew me Thy glory,* which is the natural

Ex. xxxiii. 18.

cry of every soul made for God. The answer does not indeed come as we look for it. We do not understand at first our own weakness. And so God has been pleased to make Himself known in many parts and in many fashions, by material symbol and through human Presence, as man could bear the knowledge. APP. II.

Hebr. i. 1.

By material symbol: from the Pentateuch to the Apocalypse there is one sign, one thought.

When Moses went up into the Mount to receive the tables of the Covenant, *the glory of the Lord abode on Sinai.* Ex. xxiv. 16.

When Aaron first fulfilled his priestly work of sacrifice and blessing, *the glory of the Lord appeared to all the people.* Lev. ix. 23.

When the tabernacle was completed with its sacred furniture, *the glory of the Lord filled His dwelling-place.* Ex. xl. 35.

When Solomon had dedicated the Temple and the Ark had been set in its place, *the priests could not stand to minister, for the glory of the Lord had filled the house of the Lord.* 1 Kings viii. 11.

When Ezekiel looked in a vision upon the foundations of a New Jerusalem, he saw *the glory of the Lord come into His house by the eastern gate; and behold the glory of the Lord filled the house; and he heard Him speaking unto him out of the house.* Ezek. xliii. 4 ff.

When St John beheld the Holy City descend out of heaven, he *saw no temple therein, for the* Rev. xxi. 22 f.

Lord God, the Almighty and the Lamb are the temple thereof. And the city hath no need of the sun, neither of the moon; for the glory of God did lighten it, and the lamp thereof is the Lamb.

So it was that in times of murmuring and rebellion, in times of devotion and service, God revealed His Presence by sensible signs that His people might come to recognise Him as a guiding light and a purifying fire. But no material emblem could shew truly what He is. Therefore a people, Israel, was created and fashioned for His glory, to reflect and reveal His character. And it is to the fulfilment of this national office that the prophet first looks in the words before us. The Lord, he declares, shall dawn with a great light upon Israel, and Israel shall dawn upon the world. Israel shall dawn upon the world—a renovated life shall proclaim the power of the divine spirit. A missionary nation shall prevail by righteousness. The many peoples shall turn to the centre of hope and catch its brightness. And then in a sense deeper and fuller than where mountain peak or sanctuary were crowned by a visible radiance *the glory of the Lord shall be revealed and all flesh shall see it together.*

Such was the prophet's first hope; and in this sense *the glory of the Lord* was revealed. From the date of the Return the Jews fulfilled their office as a prophetic, a Messianic nation. They embodied the truth in forms perhaps often harsh and

and in the Servant.

rigid, and visibly proclaimed that faith in the divine APP. II.
righteousness and the divine sovereignty which
the prophets had shaped. We do not, I
think, reflect sufficiently upon the grandeur of
their work. The old world has nothing to shew
like it. It was given to other races to feel after
and to unfold the broad sympathies of nature, the
subtle attractiveness of beauty, the wise discipline
of law, but the Jew received and witnessed to the
idea of holiness which is the consecration of
being. He believed, and he impressed his
belief upon all with whom he came into contact,
that our existence has a living God for its source
and for its goal. He had found the Covenant
with the Lord a reality, a spring of moral enthusiasm, a stay of resolute patience, and he enriched humanity by his knowledge.

But the meaning of the prophet is not exhausted by this national fulfilment of the promise
which he was inspired to deliver. As he draws
the brilliant picture of deliverance and spiritual
sovereignty he finds the figure of 'the servant of Is. xlii. ff.
'the Lord' occupying mysteriously the central
place. As he gazes upon the nation and
the nation's work, he is led to discern One in
Whom the blessing and the burden of Israel are
to be concentrated, One *despised and rejected* Is. liii. 3 ff.
who shall display the majesty of dominion, One
who shall shew through victorious suffering the
power and the purpose of manhood, One who

through death shall satisfy the travail of His soul. In this Figure he is able to discover some light upon the contradictions of earth: a reconciliation of the inevitable sorrows by which he is encompassed and the joys which he confidently looks for: a virtue in sacrifice reaching with spiritual force through all kindred nature: a love triumphant over ingratitude. The vision of speedy and outward success may fade away in the prospect: the necessity of righteous chastisement may be seen to rise like a dark cloud over the earth: the prophet's enthusiasm may have to encounter prevalent disbelief; but still his message gains a new intensity, a direct and personal energy. Again in this deeper, fuller meaning he cries: *the glory of the Lord shall be revealed and all flesh shall see it.*

And doubly today his words so read find for us their accomplishment. Doubly today the glory of the Lord is revealed in the Incarnation and in the Resurrection. The character of God, and the destiny of man, are laid open before us in facts which are the inexhaustible treasure of faith. Heaven and earth, earth and heaven, are shewn to be united in the fulness of one life. As today the Son of God entered the conditions of earthly life: as today the Son of man entered the conditions of heavenly life. By that descent, by that Rising, 'He has re-'vealed God to man: He has presented man to

shewn perfectly in the Life of Christ. 169

'God.' In Him—One in His essential divi- APP. II.
nity, One in the development and use of natural
powers, One in His transfigured humanity—we
can see what we are and what God is, as we
see the glory of a Father shewn in an Only John i. 14.
Son. His Life is for us the manifestation
of the Divine Nature and the Divine will: for
the present it is the assurance of power, for the
future it is a hope passing knowledge. From
first to last, in silence and prayer and teaching,
in works of power, in apparent defeats, *He mani-* John ii. 11.
*fested forth His glory—and His disciples believed
on Him.* So St John wrote of his own experience
and the words are true for all time.

For the Life of Christ, the human Life of
Christ, of which today we commemorate the beginning and the close, the ideal human life, is,
repeat, the final, the perfect revelation on
earth of the glory of God. But if that
revelation is in one sense and essentially complete,
in another sense it is still unfolded before us and
unfolded by us. The Life of Christ which consummated the ancient revelation through the Jewish
people and the Jewish prophets is now continued
in the Church and in the believer. The
glory of the Lord—we dare not shrink from the
confession—must still be revealed and the Church
and the believer are the organs of the revelation.
The Son of God hath come and hath given us 1 John v.
understanding that we may know—discern with 20.

APP. II. growing intelligence—*Him that is True.* The revelation was first made through Life, it is grasped through life, it is published through life. 'The glory of God' said an early Father 'is a living man: the life of man is the 'vision of God.' There lies the lesson of the prophet, the lesson of the day for us.

'The glory of God' which has been revealed, the glory of God which is being revealed, 'is a 'living man.' That which was shewn in Christ in all perfection without the least tinge of transitory colouring, without the least lack of abiding sympathy, we 'who are but parts' are charged to translate, as it were, through His help into forms

John i. 16. of time and place. We *receive of His fulness, grace for grace,* and it is our office by this power to read and to interpret the thoughts and the needs of our own age, to grow from point to point, to live as men who believe the message of the Annunciation and the message of Easter not as traditions but as a present Gospel: who believe that the Word became flesh, so that there is nothing truly human, however weak and perishable in present form, which is not capable of ministering to a Divine service; who believe that Jesus rose from the dead, so that there is nothing truly human, however limited and personal, which is not capable of spiritual transfigurement.

This is, we confess it with trembling hearts,

an overpowering charge, but it is our charge, APP. II. and He Who gave it will open the way to its accomplishment. To live is hard; and there is not one of us I fancy who has not again and again been tempted to despair of life when he has dared to look upon its dark mysteries; but again, there is not one of us who has not found a great sorrow, a great disappointment, a great trial, an avenue to unexpected joy. It is when we take a mean view of things, when we rest upon the surface, when we isolate ourselves proudly or sadly from the great life in which we share and to which we contribute, when we make our present powers the standard of judgment, that hope fails. But let us once come to know that the sufferings of creation are travail-pains, that Rom. viii. 22. there is an eternal meaning and purpose in the evolution of being, that there is a communion of humanity through the Communion of Saints, that when we cannot see we can rest in Him Who is holiness and love, that the blessings which mark the faith shewn as on this day are for us also: *Blessed is she that believed, for there shall* Luke i. 45. *be a fulfilment of the things which have been spoken;* and again *Blessed are they that saw not and yet believed;* and all will be changed. The glory of the Lord will be revealed, His power and His long-suffering, using and bearing with His servants.

'The glory of God is a living man; and the

172 *Lessons of the Annunciation*

APP. II.

'life of man is the vision of God.' Yes: the life of a man, and the life of a Church is the vision of God. Not always nor all at once is that sight given to us. Something at each moment is disclosed that effort may have its real foundation: something is withheld that effort may have its unfailing call. But in the Life of Christ the Son of man the vision was full, absolute, uninterrupted. That Life remains for us; and even when the light is clouded we can still look to the source whence it flows. We can keep our assurance firm by turning in every perplexity to the Gospel of this day's two-fold Festival. Can it mean less to us than that humiliation, loss, suffering, is as a veil which time casts over the fulfilment of the Divine will; that we shall find our battle won if we claim the fruits of victory; that our life, our one life, is for each of us the opportunity for so learning as men to see GOD that we may hereafter bear the transforming splendour of His open face?

1 John iii. 2.

The day encourages, or rather claims, the largest hopes, the loftiest purposes. We wrong our Faith when we do not embrace them, and confess them. It may be, as we were told three days ago, that 'we are dumb'; but if we are dumb the voice of the prophet speaks with no uncertain sound; and the vision of the prophet has not failed. The Life of Christ was not indeed universally welcomed as we should have expected. The life of the Church has been APP. II. checked and marred by many grievous maladies. The lives of believers are seen too often as isolated fragments hard to read. But none the less when we look back to the prophet's time we feel that the reality has overpassed his utmost expectation, that the glory of the Lord has been revealed and that it rests over the world.

So we look back, and we look forward. We count up, it may be, our failures, our dangers, our trials: we ask when 'the weight of custom lies 'upon us' 'Do we now believe?': we dissemble, I fear, the greatest aspirations by which we are stirred: we suspect purposes which require Divine force for execution: we remember only late that, as things are, an age is impoverished if it has no place for martyrs, for witnesses for God. But we do remember the fact on a day like this. We remember it; and then the angelic voices which we hear come back to us with a new power in the prospect of work to be done, and in the prospect of the end of work, the voice in the lowly home: *Hail thou that art* Luke i. 28. *highly favoured, the Lord is with thee:* the voice by the empty grave: *Why seek ye the* Luke xxiv. *living among the dead? He is not here: He is* 5. *risen.* With such comments, with such confirmations we can take to ourselves for our strengthening and for our consolation the promise which in past fulfilment carries the earnest of the future:

The glory of the Lord shall be revealed, and all flesh shall see it together.

'The glory of God is a living man: the life of 'man is the vision of God.'

Today that vision is opened again before our eyes.

Today that glory is again made known as the purpose of our lives.

King's College Chapel,
Easter Day, *March* 25, 1883.

APPENDIX III.

*THE REVELATION OF THE TRIUNE GOD
AN IMPLICIT GOSPEL.*

Holy, holy, holy, is the Lord God, the Almighty, which was, and which is, and which is to come.

REV. iv. 8.

The Son of God is come and hath given us an understanding that we may know Him that is true.

1 JOHN v. 20.

TODAY we are called upon to keep the festival of Revelation. Every other great festival of our Church commemorates a fact, through which God has been pleased to teach men something of His purpose of love: Trinity Sunday encourages us to reflect for a brief space on that final truth, most absolute, most elementary, most practical, which gives unity and stability to all knowledge. The view of the Divine Nature which it offers for our devout contemplation is the charter of human faith.

The festival is, as we know, of late date. It was not finally fixed on the octave of Whit Sunday till the thirteenth century (1260), and it is peculiar to the Western Church. It answers, in other words, to a late stage in the growth of the Christian society: it answers to the characteristic endowments of our own race. It seems to me to express in the highest form that striving after the vital union of the seen and unseen, which has

178 *The vision of the Divine Glory*

APP. III. added to our Creed the confession of "the Descent into Hades" and of "the Communion of Saints." Christ's work, so our Western forefathers have rejoiced to proclaim, reaches with beneficent power into the world of spirit: the fellowship of life even now is not bounded by the limits of visible intercourse: and yet more, the immovable support of human hope is the recognition of the perfect living fulness of the Being of God.

So it is that we take heart to obey the invitation which is given to us today, and to regard for a few moments the highest subject of human thought. In doing this, we follow the guidance of our services; for twice this morning we have seen, as it were, heaven opened, and caught the voice of spiritual powers. We have been
Is. vi. told how Isaiah in the prospect of the purifying
Rev. iv. afflictions of his people, how St. John in the prospect of the victorious sufferings of the Church, were allowed to look upon the Divine Majesty; and how they heard one strain, answering to deeper insight, rise from the lips of *the Seraphim* and *the living creatures*, which represent for us the sum of finite life: *Holy, holy, holy, is the Lord.* We look and listen. Sights of appalling wretchedness float before our eyes. Cries of tumultuous suffering ring in our ears. We ask whether we also may gaze on that vision and join in that hymn; and then it may be that the last words perhaps of the New Testament rise before

still offered to men.

us with a new force: *The Son of God is come and hath given us an understanding that we may know Him that is true.* That advent lays open God's judgment on good and evil, as it is involved in the Divine Nature. That advent gives us the power of an ever-increasing insight into an eternal life, and the strength of an eternal fellowship. It teaches us to wait as God waits; and in our time of waiting we can by His grace share in the angelic thanksgiving which is the expression of grateful knowledge.

To this end, however, we must use ungrudging labour. *The Son of God...hath given us an understanding that we may know...* He does not—we may say, without presumption, He cannot—give us the knowledge, but the power and the opportunity of gaining the knowledge. Revelation is not so much the disclosure of the truth as the presentment of the facts in which the truth can be discerned. It is given through life and to living men. It finds us men and it leaves us men. It is the ground of unending, untiring effort towards a larger vital apprehension of that which is laid open. It is not for the satisfaction of the intellectual part of our nature alone, but for the unfolding of our whole nature. Man was made to seek God: that is the foundation of revelation; to know Him as man: that is the condition of revelation; to grow into His likeness: that is the test of revelation.

It is obvious, I think, how these general reflections which fill our minds today, apply to the Christian conception of the Triune God. The conception was not given to us first in an abstract form. The abstract statement is an interpretation of facts, a human interpretation of vital facts, an interpretation wrought out gradually in the first years of the Church and still mastered gradually in our individual growth. We are required each in some sense to win for ourselves the inheritance which is given to us, if the inheritance is to be a blessing. We learn through the experience of history, and through the experience of life, how God acts, the Father, the Son, and the Holy Spirit, and by the very necessity of thought we are constrained to gather up these lessons into the simplest possible formula. So we come to recognise a Divine Unity, which is not sterile, monotonous simplicity; we come to recognise a Divine Trinity, which is not the transitory manifestation of separate aspects of One Person or a combination of Three distinct Beings. We come to recognise One in whom is the fulness of all conceivable existence in the richest energy, One absolutely self-sufficient and perfect, One in whom love finds internally absolute consummation, One who is in Himself a Living God, the fountain and the end of all life.

Thus we rise almost unconsciously from earth to Heaven, from the confession of what God does for us as Creator, Redeemer, Sanctifier, to the contemplation of His own Infinite Majesty, that is, from the action of God to the being of God, from the Trinity of the Christian dispensation to the Trinity of essence. And I will venture to say that the conception of God which we thus gain and which we could not have anticipated, does meet in a marvellous way the needs of men, so that it is not, as the boldness of rationalistic speculation has made it, a burden imposed upon the submission of faith, but indeed an implicit Gospel.

Our powers of thought and language are indeed very feeble, but we can both see and to some extent point out how this idea of the Father revealed through the Son, of the Son revealed through the Spirit, One God, involves no contradiction, but offers in the simplest completeness of life the union of the "one" and the "many" which thought has always striven to gain: how it preserves what we speak of as "personality" from all associations of finiteness; how it guards us from the opposite errors which are generally summed up under the terms Pantheism and Deism, the last issues of Gentile and Jewish philosophy; how it indicates the sovereignty of the Creator and gives support to the trust of the creature. We linger reverently over the conception, and we feel that the whole world is indeed a manifestation of the Triune God, yet so that He is not included in

182 *The conception of the Triune God*

APP. III. that which reflects the active energy of His love. We feel that the Triune God is Lord over the works of His will, yet so that His Presence is not excluded from any part of His Universe. We ponder that which is made
John i. 1. known to us, that when time began *the Word was with God* in the completeness of personal communion; that the life which was manifested to men
1 John i. 2. *was* already *in the beginning with the Father* realised absolutely in the Divine Essence. We contemplate this archetypal life, self-contained and self-fulfilled in the Divine Being, and we are led to believe with deep thankfulness that the finite life which flows from it by a free act of grace corresponds with the source from which it flows.

In this way it will at once appear how the conception of the Triune God illuminates the central religious ideas of the Creation and the Incarnation. It illuminates the idea of Creation. It enables us to gain firm hold of the Truth that the "becoming" which we observe under the condition of time answers to "a being" beyond time; that history is the writing out at length of that which we may speak of as a divine thought. It enables us to take up on our part the words of the four-and-twenty elders, the representatives of the whole Church, when they cast their crowns before the throne and
Rev. iv. 11. worshipped Him that sits thereon, saying, *Worthy art Thou, our Lord, and our God, to receive the*

glory and the honour and the power; for Thou didst create all things, and because of Thy will they were and were created; they were, absolutely in the ineffable depths of the mind of God, they *were created* under the limitations of earthly existence.

The same conception illuminates also the idea of the Incarnation. It enables us to see that the Incarnation in its essence is the crown of the Creation, and that man being originally made capable of fellowship with God, has in his very constitution a promise of the fulfilment of his highest destiny. It enables us to feel that the childly relation in which we stand to God has its ground in the Divine Being; and to understand that not even sin has been able to destroy the sure hope of its consummation, however sadly it may have modified in time the course by which the end is to be reached.

Following, as we have the power, such lines of thought as these, we can, I think, acknowledge thankfully that the Christian conception of the Triune God is, as I said, an implicit Gospel; that it inspires us with the sustaining conviction of a vital unity in all created things; that it brings before us the noblest, the most comprehensive, view of nature and history, as essentially the working out of a Father's will in the Son through the Spirit; that it covers, if only we will dare to trust it, all the facts of existence most completely, and welcomes the interpretation of them most

APP. III. gladly; that it enters into the life of the individual, the life of the nation, the life of the Church, and by entering into each carries them all forward to the eternal; that it gains efficacy and fulness through every development of human power; that it contains the promise of moral progress which the material world cannot itself justify; that it rises ever before us with transcendent glory, guiding us to new effort; that it hallows the simplest and commonest duties, giving personal reality to prayer and transfiguring every relationship of life.

For, as I said before, the Truth is not speculative but practical. The Christian conception of God is the translation into the language of thought of the facts of Christmas, and Easter, and Whit Sunday. By our faith in these facts we confess that the Divine Life has been united with human life; we confess, even if we do not distinctly realise the force of the confession, that the Divine Life in its absolute, inherent, ineffable perfection, is the foundation and the end of the human life. And we live, so far as life deserves the name, by this faith through which, consciously or unconsciously, we are stirred to toil and sustained in sacrifice.

Take away the facts, take away the conception which the facts quicken and shape, and what remains? Nothing, if I may speak my own mind, but a blind necessity, a movement, which even in a measurable term of years issues in the universal stillness of death. The inexorable sequence, which we call law, remains; but it is no longer the voice of One in whom we move. The darkness remains, but it is no longer as the shadow of a passing cloud, behind which the sun shines in its splendour. Every difficulty, every riddle of being remains, without the promise of relief and without the knowledge in which patience can rest unshaken.

It is, I know, most difficult to gain any real notion of life; difficult to feel what the broad sheet which tells us every morning of the past day's intrigues and strifes, joys and sorrows, sins and heroisms, births and deaths, really means; difficult to trace back the present to the past; difficult to foresee the harvest of our sowing. It is most difficult, and not often well, even to seek seriously for this vision of awful solemnity. We are children, always children; yet children who look wistfully upon a world which is for those whose eyes are opened a manifestation of our Father; and a festival like this bids us, as we can, for a brief space take in the widest view of things, that we may with clearer sight and fuller hearts *discern Him that is true*, the Living God, in whom we live, who satisfies the last wants of the soul, and thus learn a little more plainly that the "mystery," the revelation, of faith, answers to the "mystery," the revelation, of life. The vision of God is always, as it was in old time, the inspiration of the prophet; and even when the vision fades away the power which it has quickened remains, a power able, alone able, to realise a new world amidst the chaos of ruins which seems to encompass us.

Yes; the Christian conception of the Triune God is, I repeat, a message of glad tidings. And do we not too often do dishonour to the truth by accepting the position of apologists? We dwell upon the difficulties which the conception involves, difficulties which belong to the imperfection of our own powers, and not upon the Majesty which belongs to God. We are in danger of making Him dependent on the world for the satisfaction of His love. When we read that He *is* love we have found the truth; and the Truth will justify itself to him who knows what man is and what life is. Meanwhile it is given to us that we may use it as a help in striving towards the Divine likeness. That it can do this is its verification within us and without us.

And surely I need not pause to shew that it has the power. Anyone who believes, however imperfectly, that the universe with all it offers in a slow succession to his gaze is in its very nature the expression of that love which is the Divine Being and the Divine Life; who believes that the whole sum of life defaced and disfigured on the surface to our sight 'means intensely and means 'good'; who believes that the laws which he patiently traces are the expressions of a Father's will, that the manhood which he shares has been taken into God by the Son, that at every moment, in every trial, a Spirit is with him waiting to sanctify thought, and word, and deed; must in his own character receive something from the Divine glory on which he looks.

What calm reserve he will keep in face of the perilous boldness with which controversialists deal in human reasonings with things infinite and eternal. What tender reverence he will cherish towards those who have seen something of the King in His beauty. With what enthusiasm he will be kindled while he remembers that, in spite of every failure and every disappointment, his cause is won already. After what holiness he will strain while he sees the light fall about his path, that light which is fire, and knows the inexorable doom of everything which defiles.

John xvi. 33.

So we are brought back to the beginning. The revelation of God is given to us that we may be fashioned after His likeness. *The Son of God is come and hath given us an understanding that we may know Him that is true.* God first *loved us* that knowing His love we might love Him in our fellow men. Without spiritual sympathy there can be no knowledge. But where sympathy exists there is the transforming power of a divine affection. So far, therefore, as we are con-

1 John v. 20; iv. 19.

scious of a deeper life when we behold the depths of the life—the love—of God we learn even here to raise the strain of heaven: *Holy, holy, holy, is the Lord God, the Almighty, which was, and which is, and which is to come. Holy, holy, holy, is the Lord of hosts.* Our eyes are dim and our faith is weak; we behold thick clouds of misery and sin hanging over nature and men. We find no escape from their blinding, chilling, numbing vapours. But yet hope pierces through them, and ever entering afresh within the veil gains, as on this day, a vision of great joy; and then, while we regard that Will which is love, that Wisdom which is sacrifice, that Power which is holiness, we dare to look through the seen to the unseen, through the temporal to the eternal, and to complete the prophet's confession with trembling lips, casting ourselves wholly upon the revelation which interprets the longings of our soul: *Holy, holy, holy, is the Lord of Hosts: the whole earth is full of His glory.*

The fulness of the earth is His glory. May He in His great mercy grant us to see it, and seeing it to make it known.

St Mary's, Cambridge,
　　Trinity Sunday, 1883.

www.ingramcontent.com/pod-product-compliance
Lightning Source LLC
Chambersburg PA
CBHW062036220426
43662CB00010B/1522